HEALING THE HEALERS

The BYRD Model™: A Framework for Black and POC Clinicians for Somatic Trauma Healing, Rest & Liberation

Sharlisa L. Byrd, LMFT, SEP, TITC-CT, CCHT.

Byrd's Eye View Professional Counseling Solutions

For permission requests, contact:
Byrd's Eye View Professional Counseling Services (PCS)
Email: Sharlisa@byrdseyeviewpcs.org

This book is a work of nonfiction based on the author's lived experience, professional expertise, and clinical practice. Names and identifying details may have been changed to protect confidentiality.

First edition: 2026

Printed in the United States of America.

Creative & Production Team: This book was further elevated by an extraordinary creative team of Black women whose excellence, artistry, and care shaped its final form. It is a gift to create alongside women whose brilliance reflects both depth and dignity.

My heartfelt gratitude to Brandy Pelton of Word Wiser Ink Editing Lab for her editorial clarity and stewardship of this manuscript. To Markayla of Covers in Color for designing a cover that carries the strength and integrity of this work with such intention. To photographer Ariana Minor for capturing the back cover image with authenticity and presence. And to Emani Byrd for her artistry in hair and makeup, ensuring every detail reflected confidence and composure.

Creating in community like this is more than collaboration — it is celebration.

DEDICATION

To my Lord and Savior, Jesus Christ,
who met me in the breaking and called it becoming.
You turned suffering into purpose,
rest into resistance,
and pain into ministry.
May this work honor You.

This book is dedicated to my husband, Tommy, whose unwavering support has been my anchor through every challenge and triumph. Your love is my safe haven, and your belief in me gives me the courage to soar. You helped me create a sanctuary, where healing feels possible even in the hardest moments. Like the elephant, you embody wisdom and strength, always standing steady beside me.

To my beautiful daughters—Sierra, Laniesha, Ronnae, Emani, Alisa, and Shelby Love Byrd—you are my heart, my joy, and my greatest inspiration. I hope my journey reflects the transformation of a butterfly, emerging stronger and more radiant with every challenge. May you always see in yourselves the beauty, resilience, and boundless potential that I see in you.

To my precious granddaughters—Lyla, Nevada, and Liana and more to come—you are the next generation of hope and love. Your curiosity, laughter, and light remind me why I continue to fight for a world where healing and liberation are possible. You are my butterflies, and I hope this work inspires you to spread your wings and fly freely.

To my sister Talanda, and my sistas France, and Tee, thank you for the warmth and light you bring to my life. You remind me of the importance of family and the healing power of unconditional love. You've been my protectors and encouragers, holding me up when I felt I might fall.

This book is a testament to the power of connection, transformation, and love. To all who walk this journey of healing and liberation, may you find your strength, spread your wings, and remember the wisdom of the elephant and the beauty of the butterfly. Together, we fly.

Acknowledgments

This book was not written in isolation.
It was breathed into life through community
through the hands, hearts, and spirits that held me
during seasons when my own strength felt thin.

To Karen Roller, my mentor, guide, and sacred witness
thank you for standing with me through some of the hardest storms
of my life.
You saw my potential long before I could name it,
and you nurtured it with patience, compassion, and truth.
Your belief in embodied healing has shaped both my path and this work.
I am forever grateful for your presence on this journey.

To my uncle, Alton Byrd, whose excellence, humanity, and grounded
leadership
have been a blueprint for my own—
your wisdom taught me how to move through the world with dignity,
without shrinking or apologizing.
Your influence lives in every chapter of this book.

To my students at the University of San Francisco—
you kept me going when the world felt unbearably heavy.
Your brilliance, your curiosity, and your courage to show up as yourselves
reminded me why healing work matters.
You were light during the darkest season,
and your energy breathed life into these pages.

To the administrative team at the University of San Francisco—
thank you for supporting me with compassion and understanding
after my stroke.

Your kindness, flexibility, and care created the space I needed
to rest, recover, and return without fear or pressure.
In a system that doesn't always know how to hold its healers,
you did.
Your support was a balm I didn't know I needed.

To my SE community, especially my ATL Somatic Experiencing cohort—
thank you for holding me with tenderness, humor, and shared
understanding.
You offered co-regulation in its truest form,
teaching me that healing is communal, relational, and ancestral.

To my Emmanuel Baptist Church family in San Jose—
your prayers, your encouragement, your unwavering faith
carried me on days when I felt too weary to pray for myself.
Thank you, Minister Katrina Barnes and Brother Chester Hutchinson,
for standing in the gap with reverence and power.

To Jevita and Dea, who showed up with love, laughter, honesty,
and the kind of friendship that restores the nervous system—
you reminded me that sisterhood is medicine,
and that being held is as necessary as holding others.

To my professional peers, my therapist, colleagues, and clinicians of color
who shared stories, wisdom, and lived experience—
thank you for helping me shape language around our collective struggle
and our collective rising.
This book carries your voices between its lines.

To the healers, activists, and authors whose work illuminated my path—
your contributions became sacred soil for this work.

And finally, to my ancestors—
the ones whose strength I inherited,
whose resilience holds me upright,

whose whispers guided my steps even when I could not hear
them clearly—
this book is for you,
because *I am because you were.*

Thank you to every person, every prayer, every conversation,
and every moment of grace that helped bring this book into the world.
My healing is braided with yours.

FOREWORD

It's morning. Almost summer. A little girl, about seven, eight, maybe nine. She throws her feet over the side of the bed. Electricity moving through her body. Today, she has a plan. Today she is not an afterthought. Today she is included. She doesn't know what the day will take from her. She doesn't know that in hopes of reconnecting, she will build a life searching for something she doesn't yet have the language for. She will spend her career supporting others in learning to exist in a body that we learned early is not safe, teaching skills she herself is still learning to embody. And even after the degrees, the practice, the knowledge pursued in hopes of learning how to navigate her own life. She will still be fighting to exist in a system that demands everything from her. Often forgetting that we have human needs, that while she is supporting others in living, we are also trying to live.

Those are the facts of this work. We are people too. We carry the same wounds we sit with every day in our offices. We are sometimes desperately trying to learn and embody the very things we are teaching others to access. Not before. Not after we've figured it out. Literally at the same damn time. And the systems we work inside were never designed to hold us while we do it.

Sharlisa knows this. Not theoretically. Her body arrived at that conclusion before her mind even had a chance to catch up. Before the system acknowledged her. Before it even gave her the space to respond.

Sharlisa and I share something that doesn't require explanation between us. And I'm sure you understand too. We know what it is to carry wounds that came along before our credentials. We know what it means to sit across from someone else's pain while your own body is in pain, still learning what safe enough feels like. We know that the field we chose, the field we love, that in many ways chose us, was not built with our bodies in mind.

What Sharlisa has built with the BYRD Model, Belonging, Yielding, Resilience, and Disruption, is what I have been waiting for without knowing I was waiting. Not because the clinical models failed us, but because the systems we work inside constantly do. The agencies that want numbers and production over quality. The workplaces that measure output but never ask what it costs us to produce it. Sharlisa has created a framework that centers us, the healer. Not as an afterthought. Not as a self-help checklist or an Instagram post. But as a whole human whose whole body is carrying the past, the present, and the future. While simultaneously carrying the same for multiple clients.

This is lived experience transformed into framework. And it is so long overdue.

The emerging evidence on complex post-traumatic stress tells us something that would have changed my life if I had known it sooner. That integration is possible. Not just management. Not just learning to live in separate pieces. We can integrate these experiences into our lives and stop living fragmented. But that work cannot happen inside systems that treat us, the healer, as untouchable and unnoticed.

And we are no longer waiting.

Sharlisa's model makes room for what most of us have been doing in silence. Healing. Healing while we support others to heal. Grieving what we've lost while we hold space for someone else's grief. Learning to trust a body that life taught us early not to trust.

As you read this book, my hope for you is that as you embrace the remembering, you give yourself permission to pause. To notice. To practice the exercises not as assignments but as offerings to yourself. To settle. To start to heal. To recover.

I'll offer you what I offered Sharlisa. You don't have to heal alone. Do this for you. Do this with support. Claim your right to healing. Not because you've earned it, but because you are human and it has always been yours.

Keep life-ing,

Peace,

Jevita

CONTENTS

PART III: THE NERVOUS SYSTEM AS WITNESS: BREATH, OPPRESSION & LIBERATION

Part I:
The Call to Heal

Introduction
A Call to Heal the Healers

Chapter 1
Opening Reflection:
The Breaking Point and the Beginning

The room was cold, sterile, and filled with the quiet hum of machines monitoring my vitals. November 18, 2024—a date that would forever mark the moment my body forced me to stop. The moment of my rebirth. I lay in the emergency room, unable to move the right side of my body, unable to grasp what had just happened. A stroke. At work. In the very institution that preached healing, but had slowly been breaking me down.

It wasn't my patients who had drained me. It wasn't the stories of trauma I had held space for, or the weight of their pain that I carried with me long after our sessions ended. No, the real wound had been inflicted by the very system I had devoted my life to. The microaggressions that chipped away at my confidence, the subtle yet persistent questioning of my competence, the outright acts of racism that I was expected to endure with grace. The long hours, the impossible demands, the gaslighting when I named the harm—it had all culminated in this moment. My body had been whispering, then speaking, then screaming at me to slow down, to pay attention, to choose myself. And when I didn't listen, it chose for me.

As I lay there, staring at the ceiling, a wave of realization washed over me. I had spent years advocating for my patients, teaching my students, showing up for my family—yet I had abandoned myself. I had ignored my body's pleas, suppressing the anxiety, the exhaustion, the deep knowing that something had to change. My body had kept the score, and now, it was demanding something different.

This was my reckoning. The moment I knew I could no longer wait for these systems to become just, for my humanity to be recognized, for someone else to grant me permission to rest. The healing I had been offering to others—I had to claim it for myself. This was not just about survival. This was about reclamation. It was about breaking the cycle of harm that had been passed down for generations, about honoring my ancestors by refusing to be consumed by the very structures they had fought against.

That hospital bed became my altar of awakening. I made a promise to myself that day—not just to recover, but to *reclaim*. My body, my mind, my spirit. My joy. My peace. My purpose.

This book is born from that promise. A promise to tell the truth about what it means to be a Black clinician in systems not built for our survival. A promise to offer the tools that helped me crawl back to myself. A promise to hold space for every healer who has ever felt invisible, undervalued, and unseen. Because we are not meant to just survive—we are meant to *thrive*.

The Unspoken Battle: Systemic Challenges for Black Clinicians

I entered this field to be a healer, to help others navigate their deepest wounds, to create spaces where people could feel seen, heard, and understood. But what I was not prepared for—what no training program could have prepared me for—was how often I would have to fight to be seen myself.

Being a Black clinician in systems not built for us means constantly carrying a weight that others do not. For Black clinicians and social workers, these changes feel deeply personal. We know how hard we have worked to carve out spaces where we and our communities feel seen and valued. Black clinicians make up only a small fraction of the mental health workforce—a sliver of psychologists, an even smaller presence among psychiatrists, and far too few LMFTs and social workers. This scarcity places an outsized weight on our shoulders, asking us to hold the needs of Black clients who are searching for clinicians who care and truly understand them. We are stretched thin not because we lack brilliance or commitment, but because the system was never built with us in mind, nor built to sustain us. Without Diversity, Equity, and Inclusion (DEI) protections, that gap will only widen, leaving Black clients even more vulnerable in a mental health system that has historically overlooked them. But perhaps the deepest wound comes from the message these rollbacks send to our communities— that our pain, our trauma, our healing are somehow not priorities. That the progress we've made is disposable. The labor we have done to educate, uplift, and create equitable care can simply be erased.

And yet, we are still here. This disparity underscores the urgent need to increase the number of Black mental health practitioners to provide culturally responsive care and address the unique mental health challenges faced by Black communities. It means watching your expertise be questioned while your white colleagues receive praise for doing less. It means sitting in meetings where your ideas are ignored, only for them to be repeated by someone else minutes later and suddenly deemed brilliant. It means knowing that when you advocate for yourself, when you set boundaries, when you challenge injustice, you risk being labeled "angry," "difficult," or "unprofessional, or having limited understanding." It means showing up to do the work of healing while simultaneously enduring the very harms you are helping your patients process.

I have lived this reality. I have been dismissed, gaslit, and excluded from opportunities that were readily handed to my peers. I have been told to "just focus on the work" when I voiced concerns about racism in the workplace. I have sat across from supervisors who ignored my health concerns, belittled my attempts to advocate for myself, and made decisions that eroded my ability to perform at my best. I have held my breath as patients questioned my competence simply because of the color of my skin, while those in power expected me to accept it as part of the job.

And my story is not unique. This is the lived experience of so many Black clinicians who dedicate themselves to a system that refuses to fully see them. Research shows that Black therapists routinely face racial bias, discrimination, and subtle forms of gatekeeping within the very systems where we are expected to heal others. These repeated wounds don't just bruise our spirits; they accumulate, increasing stress, deepening burnout, and pushing many Black clinicians out of the field long before their gifts have fully blossomed. We enter this work to heal, yet the environments we work within often leave us wounded.

For years, I believed I could endure it. That if I just worked harder, proved myself more, stayed quiet when I wanted to speak up, I could make it through. But my body knew the truth long before I did. Our bodies are the first place we learn what it means to feel joy, love, connection, and safety, and they are also the chambers where our fear and pain quietly take root. Long before we speak the story, the body carries it. It remembers everything we've lived through, the sweetness and the sorrow, holding it all in its own language beneath the skin. The stress, the erasure, the constant hypervigilance—it was all taking root inside me, manifesting as anxiety, fatigue, and, eventually, the stroke that forced me to stop.

But stopping did not mean surrendering. It meant finally listening. It meant realizing that my survival—my ability to continue this work—was dependent on finding a new way forward. That new way was not through enduring more harm but through reclaiming my body, my boundaries, my voice, and my right to heal.

This book centers my unique experiences as a Black clinician, acknowledging the particular challenges and strengths within this group. At the same time, it recognizes that the journey of healing, resilience, and advocacy is shared across the entire BIPOC community. The wisdom, struggles, and victories of Indigenous, Latinx, Asian, Pacific Islander, and other people of color clinicians are woven throughout, as we stand united in the fight for justice, equity, and healing for all. This book is about that reclamation. It is about the somatic tools that helped me reconnect with myself when the weight of systemic harm had left me numb. It is about the power of community, of ancestral wisdom, of unapologetically prioritizing our well-being. It is about refusing to let systems of oppression define us, shrink us, or silence us.

To every Black and POC clinician who has ever felt unseen, unheard, or unprotected within these systems—this book is for you. Not just as a guide for navigating the harm but as a map toward liberation. Because we are not here to just survive. We are here to *thrive*.

A Time for Advocacy and Resilience

The results are in. The votes have been counted. And yet, no matter which administration holds power, one truth remains unchanged: justice does not wait. Healing does not pause. The systemic inequities embedded within healthcare, mental health, and education do not suddenly disappear with the shifting tides of political leadership.

For Black and POC clinicians, this reality is both deeply personal and profoundly collective. We do not have the luxury of disengaging because our existence itself is an act of resistance. Every session we hold, every client we guide toward healing, every space we take up in institutions that were never designed for us—these are acts of advocacy. They are declarations that we belong, that we matter, and that we will not be erased.

The next four years will bring change, though we do not yet know in what form. Perhaps there will be new policies aimed at dismantling the barriers we face. Perhaps there will be renewed efforts to suppress our voices, to make us smaller, to push us back into silence. What we do know is this: we must be prepared. We must remain vigilant, not only in the fight for justice but in the fight for our own well-being.

As I sit back, feeling helpless as DEI programs are dismantled and Black history is erased from schools, I am reminded that the work I do is more critical than ever. The erasure of our stories, our contributions, and our struggles is not just an attack on history—it is an attack on our collective healing. The dismantling of DEI initiatives across the country is more than a policy shift; it is a direct attack on the work so many of us have poured our hearts into. It sends a chilling message to Black therapists, clinicians of color, and mental health professionals that the spaces we fought to make more inclusive are being taken from us. A recent federal order eliminating DEI programs across government agencies has wiped out vital streams of funding, mentorship, and professional support. For Black and Brown mental health providers, this means resources that once helped us enter, remain in, and grow within the field are vanishing. The doors that were only beginning to open are now being pushed shut again—not because the need has lessened, but because the systems meant to support equity are being dismantled in plain sight. Across the corporate world, major companies have begun pulling back on their diversity hiring commitments. As these goals shrink, so do the pathways that once offered hope for Black therapists and therapists of color. Opportunities that were slowly beginning to widen are narrowing again, making it even more challenging to enter spaces where our presence, perspective, and expertise are desperately needed.

Civil Unrest: A New Layer of Trauma

As we witness a new wave of upheaval across our nation, particularly in cities like Los Angeles, Portland, New Orleans, Washington, DC, Minneapolis, Raleigh, Durham, Chapel Hill, and Chicago, we are reminded that systemic violence takes many forms—some more visible than others— but all equally damaging to the fabric of our communities. Recently, the increasing presence of ICE raids, coupled with the deployment of the National Guard, has sparked both fear and resistance within immigrant and marginalized communities. Families are once again forced to live in the shadows, unsure of where safety lies or whether their children will come home from school.

The trauma of being pursued, of being told your presence is unwelcome, is a silent burden carried on the shoulders of those who live with the constant fear of deportation, displacement, and separation from loved ones. These raids do not just break up families; they break the spirit of a community. They chip away at the belief that we all belong here and have a right to safety, dignity, and life.

For those of us who provide care to these communities, the emotional toll is profound. The stress from living under constant surveillance, the anxiety of not knowing what will happen tomorrow, the grief of witnessing people's lives and futures being torn apart—these are the realities many of our clients face daily. As mental health providers, we find ourselves in the impossible position of offering healing while the very structures that need healing are tearing at the seams.

But even in the face of these terrifying realities, we see resilience. We see mothers marching in the streets, demanding their right to care for their children. We see communities gathering in solidarity, refusing to let fear silence them. We see organizers and advocates working tirelessly to dismantle systems that separate and oppress. Their work is an embodiment of hope, and it is our responsibility to stand alongside them both as providers of care and as advocates for justice.

The social unrest we are witnessing is not just a fight against policies that tear apart families. It is a fight for our collective humanity. It is a fight that reminds us of the intersectionality of oppression—how the struggles of Black, Brown, and Indigenous communities are often compounded by economic disparity, racial violence, and now, the weaponization of immigration enforcement.

As the National Guard and ICE disrupt communities, it is not just the immigrants or the refugees who are affected; it is all of us. It is a trauma that ripples out, a reminder that the fight for justice is not one that we can afford to sit out. Just as we heal, we must also rise in resistance, holding onto the belief that the right to safety, to freedom, and to dignity is not a privilege for the few—it is a birthright for all.

In this moment of unrest, we must remind ourselves that healing, advocacy, and resistance are not separate; they are intertwined. It is in the act of standing firm against oppression that we also honor our own healing. It is in the act of loving and caring for our communities that we fight for justice.

Even in the face of systemic opposition, we continue to show up for our clients, our students, our communities, and ourselves. Even without formal DEI structures, we continue to find ways to connect, uplift, and build spaces of healing. Because we have always done this work not for validation, not for institutional approval, but because our people deserve care.

I grieve what is being lost, but I also hold tightly to what cannot be taken— our resilience, our wisdom, our unwavering commitment to creating healing spaces. We have always found ways to thrive in systems that were not built for us, and we will continue to do so. But this moment calls for something more: it calls for us to care for ourselves as fiercely as we care for others. It calls for us to hold onto one another, to continue the work, and to remind ourselves that we are not alone in this fight.

The message is that our pain is not real, that our resilience is not worth honoring. But we know better. Our ancestors carried this fight long before us, and now, it is our turn to ensure that the next generation does not grow up in a world where their history and humanity are deemed expendable.

Advocacy is not just about protesting in the streets or speaking on panels; it is also about survival. It is about knowing when to push and when to rest, when to speak and when to listen to the wisdom within. It is about recognizing that our ability to care for others is directly tied to our ability to care for ourselves. Caring for ourselves is far more than a luxury; it is a necessary act of survival. For those of us living in bodies the world tries to diminish, tending to our well-being becomes a bold declaration that we will not be erased. Self-care, in this context, is resistance. It is how we stay alive, whole, and rooted in our power.

This is the moment to reclaim our breath, our space, and our right to healing. To stand firm in our expertise and demand the respect we have long been denied. To use our voices not only to advocate for others but to ensure that we are heard, valued, and protected in the spaces where we work and serve.

The road ahead is uncertain, but one thing is clear: we will not walk it alone. We will move forward together, rooted in the power of community, the wisdom of our ancestors, and the unshakable belief that justice is not a request. It is a birthright. And we will claim it.

CHAPTER 2
THE JOURNEY AHEAD:
THE BYRD MODEL

This book is more than just my story—it is a testimony to the weight of care, the cost of resilience, and the urgent need for healing. It is a reflection of the struggles I have endured as a Black clinician navigating workplaces that questioned my expertise, silenced my voice, and demanded my labor while denying my worth. It is also a tribute to those who came before me, the ancestors who carried the fight for justice in their bones, and the communities who continue to rise despite the barriers placed before them.

For years, I pushed through the microaggressions, the dismissals, and the systemic hurdles, believing that if I just worked harder, I would be seen. But the truth is, these systems were never designed for us to thrive. They were built to diminish, to exhaust, to extract until there is nothing left to give. And I gave until my body, weary from years of unprocessed pain, finally demanded that I listen.

Healing, I have learned, is not just an intellectual process. It is a renovation of the body, a returning to the wisdom that has always lived within us. Through Somatic Experiencing, breathwork, ancestral rituals, and the BYRD Model, I began to reweave the connection between my body and spirit, unlearning the survival mechanisms that had kept me in a constant state of overdrive. I created cultural meditations that resonated with my multifaceted identity, seeking refuge in the traditions of my people: prayer, movement, and collective storytelling. I learned to speak my needs aloud, to honor what my body was telling me, and to no longer shrink myself for systems that thrived on my silence.

But my story is not finished. Healing is not a destination; it is a continuous, evolving practice. I do not claim to have all the answers, but what I do know is this: we cannot heal in isolation. And so, I invite you to walk this path with me.

Together, we will explore how trauma lives in the body and how somatic healing can help us release what no longer serves us. We will name the injustices we face, not as an act of despair but as an act of liberation. We will reflect, reclaim, and reimagine a world where our well-being is not an afterthought but a priority.

This book is a space for validation, empowerment, and transformation. It is a call to honor your body, your voice, and your truth. Because in a world that too often seeks to silence and erase us, our greatest act of defiance is to heal, to thrive, and to take up space unapologetically.

What This Book Offers

This book is a deeply personal invitation into the realities of being a Black clinician in systems not built for us to thrive. While this work centers on Black clinicians, the insights shared here also resonate with BIPOC clinicians who navigate similar challenges across different cultural contexts. It is a space where truth is spoken—where the weight of microaggressions, racial bias, and workplace harassment is named, not as a burden to bear in silence, but as something to be witnessed, processed, and transformed. I share my own stories of the injustices that pushed me to the brink and the somatic practices that helped me reclaim my power. I will introduce my BYRD Model that was created out of love, longing, and the desire to heal. You will not just read about systemic racism in mental health spaces, you will learn how these injustices embed themselves into our nervous systems, how they take up space in our bodies, and how tools like Polyvagal Theory, breathwork, Judith Herman's Tri-Phasic Model of Trauma Resolution Somatic Experiencing, and The BYRD Model can help us shift from merely surviving to actively healing.

This book is for Black clinicians and anyone who has ever felt unseen, unheard, or undervalued in their professional spaces. It is for those who give so much of themselves to others while being denied the care, recognition, and support they deserve. It is for those who are carrying more than they should, who are burning out in the name of resilience, and who need permission to pause, to feel, and to reclaim their voice and their body. Healing is possible, not just for our patients but for us as the healers.

Introducing the BYRD Model: A Framework for Trauma Healing and Liberation

As I reflected on my own journey and the profound impact that systemic trauma had on my body and mind, I realized that traditional approaches to healing often fell short. Healing from trauma, especially the kind of generational and systemic trauma many of us face as Black and BIPOC clinicians, requires a framework that honors not only the individual but the collective. The BYRD Model is that framework, a holistic guide to navigating trauma, reclaiming our power, and ultimately achieving liberation.

I created the BYRD Model because traditional trauma treatment models did not speak my language, the language of embodied pain, ancestral wisdom, and surviving systems that were never built for us. I created it because I saw brilliant, exhausted, trauma-carrying students falling through the cracks of institutions that offered policy instead of presence. This model was born out of necessity, a reclamation of healing. It offers a pathway that is body-based, justice-driven, and rooted in the cultural wisdom of those it serves. It invites students, clients, clinicians, educators, and the community to not just treat trauma, but to transform the very systems that perpetuate it.

The BYRD Model did not arrive as a theory; it came as a whisper, then a roar. It rose from the space between collapse and awakening, where my body finally demanded truth. What began as survival became revelation:

healing could no longer mean enduring; it had to mean returning to the body, to community, to the sacred rhythm of rest.

The Birth of the Model: From Breakdown to Breakthrough

The BYRD Model was not born in a classroom, a research lab, or a board meeting.

It was born in stillness, in the sterile hum of a hospital room where my body finally spoke the truth my mouth had been too afraid to say.

For years, I had carried the weight of injustice like armor. I had worn professionalism as protection, compassion as a currency that cost me my own breath. The strokes of racism and overwork came not in one brutal blow, but in a thousand quiet betrayals, every time I smiled through harm, every time I said, "I'm fine" while my body whispered, *You are not.*

And then, one day, my body stopped whispering.
It demanded my attention.

As I lay there, half-paralyzed but fully awake, I realized that I had been healing everyone but myself. I had given voice to others' pain but silenced my own. My nervous system—that quiet, faithful witness to every microaggression, every dismissal, every exhaustion—had reached its threshold.

It was in that sacred pause that something ancient rose up in me. A knowing. A remembering.
Healing could no longer mean simply patching the wounds that systems kept reopening. It had to mean *reclaiming the body*, remembering what had been dismembered, and returning to the wisdom we carry in our blood.

The BYRD Model came to me as both revelation and instruction—not as a theory to be taught, but as a truth to be lived.

Each letter—Belonging, Yielding, Resilience, and Disruption—arrived as a rhythm, a cycle of healing that mirrors the body's own way of processing pain and returning to balance.
It is a framework, yes, but more than that, it is a way of being.
It is how we remember ourselves whole again.

The BYRD Model is built upon four essential principles that create a path toward liberation, healing, and resilience:

Belonging: The Medicine of Being Seen

Belonging is where healing begins.
Before we can release trauma, before we can rebuild resilience, we must have a place to land, a place where the body and the soul both whisper, *You are safe here.*

For too long, those of us in Black and Brown bodies have been asked to survive in systems that see our labor but not our light. We have learned to earn our belonging through overwork, through silence, through shapeshifting into versions of ourselves that fit the comfort of others. But that is not belonging; that is *performance.*

True belonging is not granted by institutions; it is reclaimed within the body. It is the moment your nervous system exhales and says, *I can be here as I am.*

When we belong, our cells unclench.
When we belong, our breath deepens.
When we belong, the body remembers joy.

Belonging is the soil in which liberation grows.

It is the medicine that allows us to be both soft and strong, to exist without apology.

In my own journey, I had mistaken inclusion for belonging.
I thought being invited to the table meant I was seen, until I realized the table was built on our silence.
Belonging, I learned, means building our own table. It means looking around the room and finding those who see you not for what you can produce, but for who you *are*.
It means trusting that your body, your story, and your truth deserve to take up space.

Somatic Invitation

- Place one hand over your heart, one over your belly.

- Breathe in slowly through your nose, and as you exhale, whisper: *I belong here.*

- Notice what shifts, the weight of your shoulders, the rhythm of your breath, the warmth beneath your palms.

- Let your body teach you what safety feels like.

Reflection

- Where in your life do you feel most seen?

- Where do you still feel invisible, and why have you stayed there?

- What would it mean to build a space, internally or externally, where you no longer have to shrink?

Belonging is the foundation of the BYRD Model because safety is the gateway to transformation.
You cannot heal what you must hide.
You cannot rest in a space that asks you to disappear.
Belonging is the radical act of returning to yourself, the first and fiercest form of freedom.

Yielding: The Sacred Art of Rest

Yielding is the breath between battles.
It is the pause after the body has fought too long to stay upright.
It is the sacred moment when we remember that stillness, too, is a form
of survival.

For so many of us, especially those who live and work in systems that
demand our constant proving, rest feels dangerous. We are taught to
equate our worth with our productivity, our healing with our hustle.
Even as clinicians and caretakers, we push through exhaustion, convincing
ourselves that fatigue is just another badge of service. But the body
knows better.

The body keeps the receipts.
The body knows that rest is not the absence of progress—it is the soil that
growth requires.

Yielding is not giving up; it is giving *in*.
It is letting go of the grip that trauma taught us to hold. It is the slow,
holy exhale after years of bracing. It is what happens when the nervous
system finally receives permission to unclench.

When I was recovering from my stroke, I had to relearn what it
meant to yield.
Every instinct in me wanted to push, rehabilitate faster, get back to teaching, get back to "doing." But my body was firm: *No more pushing. No
more pretending.*
Yielding meant learning to trust my own slow return, to surrender to rest
as medicine rather than punishment. I learned that the body heals not
when we force it, but when we listen to it.

Yielding asks us to recognize that slowing down is not a failure of will-
power; it is a reclamation of rhythm.
Our ancestors did not survive by moving faster; they survived by knowing

when to pause, when to breathe, when to honor the cycles of day and night, giving and receiving. Rest, in their wisdom, was not optional; it was sacred.

When we yield, we turn toward that ancestral memory. We begin to soften into ourselves.
We make space for our parasympathetic system, the body's built-in balm, to come forward and remind us that safety lives in stillness.

In this culture of relentless motion, yielding is rebellion.
It says: *My worth is not tied to my productivity.*
It says: *I refuse to be consumed by systems that thrive on my exhaustion.*
It says: *I choose myself.*

To yield is to listen to the body's whisper before it has to scream.

Somatic Invitation

- Find a comfortable seated position or lie flat on your back.
- Inhale deeply, filling your belly with air.
- As you exhale, imagine laying down every burden you've been carrying: the expectations, the deadlines, the guilt.
- Repeat this phrase softly: *It is safe to rest.*
- Notice what your body does when it finally believes you.

Reflection

- What does your body say when you try to rest? Does it resist, fidget, bargain?
- Where did you first learn that rest was dangerous, lazy, or selfish?
- How might your healing change if you began to see stillness as a form of power?

Yielding is not weakness; it is wisdom.
It is the body's way of saying, *You have done enough for today.*

It is the quiet knowing that restoration is revolutionary.
When we yield, we stop performing strength and start embodying it.
We stop running and start arriving.

Yielding is the sacred art of letting go, of loosening the armor that no
longer fits, of releasing the myth that we must earn our right to breathe.
In this release, we meet the deepest kind of healing: not the kind that
demands movement, but the kind that whispers, *Be still. You have survived. Now, rest.*

Resilience: Remembering Our Inherited Strength

Resilience is the pulse of our lineage.
It is not a skill we learned; it is a rhythm we inherited.
Every breath we take today carries the memory of those who came before
us, those who survived enough storms to give us a name, a heartbeat,
and a story.

For too long, resilience has been misunderstood.
It has been twisted into the expectation that we must always rise, always
push through, always smile through the ache. But true resilience is not
about bouncing back; it is about *rooting deeper*.
It is not a demand; it is a remembrance.

Resilience is not born in the absence of pain, but in the presence
of purpose.
It does not ask us to harden—it invites us to expand.
It teaches us that strength is not stoicism, and that survival is not the
same as healing.

When I began to reclaim my own resilience, I realized it had never left
me. It was braided into my DNA—the laughter of my mother Polly, even
when bills were due; the prayer of my grandmother Polly whispered over
a pot of beans; the way my daughters hold one another when the world

feels too heavy.

Resilience lives in our gestures, our humor, our community, our dance. It lives in the way we still find beauty in a world that tries to make us forget it exists.

Resilience is the nervous system learning to *return*.
It is the ventral vagal hum of connection that says, *I am not alone.*
It is the body's memory of safety resurfacing after generations of bracing.
It is joy as an act of defiance.

I have learned that resilience is not about erasing pain—it is about transforming it.
When we cry, the body metabolizes grief.
When we laugh, it recalibrates toward hope.
When we breathe fully, we teach our descendants that peace is possible.

Resilience asks us to stay tender in a world that rewards the hardened.
It asks us to stay open when we have every reason to close.
It asks us to believe that our healing ripples forward—that each act of care, each boundary set, each moment of rest, is a gift to those who will come after.

Somatic Invitation

- Place your feet on the ground and press them gently into the earth.

- Feel your spine lengthen, your chest open.

- Inhale through your nose, exhale through your mouth, and whisper: *I come from resilience.*

- Notice any sensations that arise—warmth, tingling, tears, a sense of steady power.

- Let them move through you without needing to fix or manage them.

Reflection

- What does resilience mean to you when you remove the pressure to "be strong"?

- Who taught you resilience—not by words, but by the way they lived?

- What ancestral strengths are waiting to be remembered in your body today?

Resilience is not new; it is remembered.

It is the sacred inheritance that trauma tried to bury but could never kill.

When we honor our resilience, we honor those who survived long enough for us to rest.

When we embody it, we become living proof that healing does not end with us—it continues through us.

Resilience is the bridge between what was broken and what will be born.

It is the quiet strength that whispers beneath every heartbeat:

You are your ancestors' answered prayer.

Disruption: Liberation as Healing

Disruption is the fire that follows the breath.

It is the tremor that shakes the ground after years of holding still.

It is the sacred refusal to keep participating in what harms us.

For too long, healing has been confused with politeness.

We have been told to stay calm, stay quiet, stay professional, even in the face of systems that deplete and dehumanize us. But the body knows: silence can be a trauma response. Compliance can be a cage.

True healing cannot happen without truth-telling, and truth-telling is always disruptive.

Disruption is not destruction.
It is creation.
It is what happens when something inside us says, *No more pretending.*
When we stop negotiating for our humanity and start embodying it.

For me, disruption came through collapse.
My body, my truest ally, rebelled against injustice before my mind could.
It stopped me, forced me to listen, and in doing so, became my greatest teacher. My stroke was my body's protest, a sacred strike against overwork, racism, and self-abandonment. It was not the end; it was initiation.

Disruption begins in the body long before it reaches the boardroom or the streets.
It starts as a tremor in the gut, a tightening in the chest, a moment of dizziness when the soul whispers, *You are out of alignment.*
To honor that whisper is to become dangerous in the best way, because systems of oppression depend on our disconnection. When we reconnect, we dismantle.

Disruption is not just saying "no"; it is saying "yes" to something truer.
Yes to integrity.
Yes to wholeness.
Yes to liberation that begins within and radiates outward.

When we disrupt, we make room for what is sacred.
We reclaim the space where our joy, our rage, and our rest can coexist.
We model to our clients, our students, and our children that healing is not about fitting in—it's about transforming what we've been forced to adapt to.

Disruption is the bridge between healing and justice.
It is the moment the body says, *I will no longer participate in my own suppression.*
It is the reclamation of voice, of time, of rhythm.

And it is not always loud.
Sometimes disruption is as simple as saying no without apology.
Sometimes it's leaving the meeting early to take a walk.
Sometimes it's calling a thing by its true name.
Sometimes it's rest, laughter, or softness in a world that expects you to stay armored.

Disruption is liberation in motion, the body returning to its natural rhythm after centuries of forced containment.

Somatic Invitation

- Sit or stand tall and take a deep breath.

- As you exhale, imagine shedding the layers of expectation, professionalism, and perfection that do not belong to you.

- Feel your feet on the ground, your spine alive, your shoulders open.

- Say out loud or whisper: *My healing is disruptive.*

- Notice what power begins to rise from within.

Reflection

- What does it mean for you to disrupt without destroying yourself?

- Where in your life or work are you being called to speak truth, even if your voice shakes?

- How might you honor the small rebellions, rest, boundaries, softness, as acts of liberation?

Disruption is the thunder after generations of quiet.
It is the body reclaiming its voice, the spirit remembering its worth.
When we disrupt, we do not reject our humanity; we return to it.
We become living resistance, grounded in love, rooted in integrity, and guided by the knowing that liberation is not a theory; it's a rhythm we remember.

When we embody Belonging, Yielding, Resilience, and Disruption, we do

not just heal; we transform.
We become both the medicine and the movement.

The Flight: A BYRD Manifesto for Healing

Belonging taught me to come home to my body.
Yielding taught me to rest there.
Resilience reminded me that I am not the first to rise, and I will not be the last.
Disruption whispered that healing and justice are not separate; they are the same heartbeat.

This is what it means to be a BYRD.
To belong, even when the world tries to unsee you.
To yield, even when the culture demands your constant motion.
To remember resilience as inheritance, not performance.
To disrupt, even when your voice trembles, because silence has never kept us safe.

Healing is not linear; it's cyclical, like breath, like prayer, like flight.
We descend into stillness so that we may rise with intention.
We gather our broken pieces not to return to who we were, but to become who we are meant to be.

The BYRD Model is not a method—it's a movement.
It is an invitation to return to our bodies, our boundaries, and our belonging.
It is a map back to ourselves, written in breath, in heartbeat, in lineage.

When we practice Belonging, we re-root.
When we practice Yielding, we rest.
When we practice Resilience, we remember.
When we practice Disruption, we rise.

We are not broken; we are becoming.

We are not fragile; we are remembering our flexibility.
We are not too much; we are exactly as vast as we were designed to be.

So, to every healer who has been told to shrink,
to every therapist who has carried the weight of generations while being
asked to smile through it,
to everybody who has trembled under the pressure to perform strength
this is your permission slip to exhale.

Rest.
Reclaim.
Rise.

You do not heal alone.
You heal in rhythm.
You heal in community.
You heal in motion.

And when you do, when you dare to belong, yield, rise, and disrupt
you do not just heal yourself.
You heal the system that forgot how to breathe.

The BYRD Model begins with the body, but it does not end there; it
ripples outward, touching our clients, our classrooms, our families, and
our collective future. This is the work of healing the healers: one nervous
system, one truth, one breath at a time.

Chapter 3
Understanding the Terrain

Opening Reflection

The weight of being a mental health clinician is heavy. Every day, we step into the most vulnerable parts of people's lives, holding space for their grief, trauma, and healing, while often neglecting the weight we ourselves carry. For Black clinicians, however, this burden is compounded by the systemic injustices woven into the very institutions we serve. We are expected to show up as healers, yet we are often navigating our own wounds inflicted by the very systems in which we work.

As a professor, I feel this weight even more deeply. I watch my BIPOC students step into a field that was not built with them in mind. I see their passion, their dedication, their brilliance, and I know that many of them will soon face challenges that extend beyond patient care. They will experience the sting of having their competence questioned, the exhaustion of code-switching, the discomfort of being the only person of color in the room, and the heartbreak of advocating for justice in spaces that were never designed to accommodate them. I want to prepare them for this reality, but how do you teach someone to endure harm that should not exist in the first place?

This dual role, clinician and educator, often feels like walking a tightrope. I carry the stories of my patients and my students, their hopes and fears pressed against my own. But it is in this balance that I find purpose. The weight of care is heavy, but it is also transformative. It has taught me that healing is not about fixing what is broken; it is about creating space for what is possible. It is about recognizing that while we have been conditioned to endure and persist, we also have the right to rest, to feel, to heal.

And this is where the BYRD Model becomes not just a tool for personal healing, but a guide for helping my students navigate the weight they will carry in their own careers. Through Belonging, they will learn the importance of creating safe spaces, spaces where they can be seen and valued for who they are, not for who they are expected to be. Through Yielding, they will understand that rest is resistance, and that self-care is not selfish but essential to their well-being. In Resilience, they will find strength in their cultural heritage, recognizing that their ancestors' wisdom is embedded in them, propelling them forward even in the face of adversity. Finally, Disruption will remind them that while they may face systemic obstacles, they also have the power to challenge and transform these systems, making space for themselves and others to thrive.

By introducing the BYRD Model into their training, I aim to equip them not only with clinical skills but also with the tools to reclaim their own power, to advocate for their own healing, and to disrupt the systems that will try to limit their own potential.

The weight of care is not just professional; it is deeply personal. It is the long hours spent giving everything to others, only to be overlooked when it is time for promotions. It is the exhaustion of witnessing inequities go unaddressed, while being expected to quietly bear them. It is the frustration of having to work twice as hard to receive half the recognition. It is knowing that, in many workplaces, our expertise will be questioned, our voices will be dismissed, and our well-being will be deprioritized.

This weight doesn't stay tucked neatly in the mind; it sinks into the body. Trauma makes its home in our muscles, our breath, our posture, the quiet places we rarely name. The body holds the truths we try to outrun, and in the end, it speaks louder than our thoughts. It carries the story long after the moment has passed, insisting that we listen. I have felt this truth firsthand. The exhaustion I carried did not just stay in my thoughts; it seeped into my muscles, my breath, my nervous system. I ignored the tension in my shoulders, the persistent headaches, the sleepless nights. I convinced myself that if I just pushed a little harder, endured a little longer, things would get better. But the body keeps score. My body kept track of every dismissal, every moment of being overlooked, every time I swallowed my pain instead of speaking up.

Eventually, it all became too much. On November 18, 2024, my body forced me to listen. I suffered a stroke at work, right before seeing a patient who had expressed racist views toward the BIPOC community in every session. A patient I had been told to continue seeing, because my discomfort was dismissed as a "learning experience" rather than the emotional harm it truly was. That day, my body said, *enough.* My nervous system, which had been in survival mode for so long, could no longer sustain the weight.

This is the cost of carrying the weight of care in a system that does not care for us.

As I reflect on my journey, I realize that this weight is not just mine to carry; it is one that so many Black and BIPOC clinicians bear. The stress, the burnout, the mental and physical toll—it is not an individual failure, but a systemic crisis. It is a sign that the very institutions that claim to promote healing are often the ones causing the most harm.

This chapter is a call to name this weight, to acknowledge its impact, and to explore how we can move toward healing, not just for ourselves, but for those who will follow in our footsteps.

Chapter 4
The Body as Compass,
Learning to Listen
Again

Before we can heal others, we must learn the language of our own bodies. Not the language of diagnoses or DSM categories, but the language of sensation, breath, rhythm, and rest.

The body is not the obstacle to our healing.
It is the map.

In the Western world, we have been conditioned to treat the body as something to control or silence. Even in our profession, we talk about "regulation" as if the body were a machine needing adjustment instead of a sacred ecosystem longing for connection.

The body is the first text we ever read.
The first prayer we ever spoke.

But trauma disrupts that knowing.
It teaches the nervous system to brace instead of breathe, to tense instead of trust. And yet, even in trauma, the body keeps searching for safety. It whispers through:

- a tightening in the chest

- a trembling in the hands

- an ache behind the eyes

When we learn to listen, we realize the body has been telling the story all along.

The Body Remembers, and So Must We

I have sat with clients who can explain their trauma with clinical precision yet feel nothing in their bodies. They speak insight fluently but flinch at an invitation to breathe.

That distance is not defiance; it is protection.

It is the body doing exactly what it learned to do: survive.

As we gently restore connection, the body becomes a truth-teller. It tells us:

- when we're safe
- when we're stretching too far
- when numbness is showing up as "calm"

The body becomes the compass that leads us back to belonging.

Somatic Literacy: A New Kind of Knowing

To heal the healers, we must teach somatic literacy
the capacity to read the body like sacred scripture:

slowly
reverently
with humility

Somatic literacy means knowing the difference between:

- calm and collapse
- safety and suppression
- groundedness and guarding

This is not theory; it is practice.

It lives in:

- the breath you take before entering a session
- the unclenching of the jaw while you grade papers
- the moment you pause before saying "yes" when your body already whispered "no"

We cannot co-regulate from disconnection.
We cannot model safety from self-neglect.

When we embody grounding, our presence becomes pedagogy.
Our regulation becomes medicine.

Reflection Questions

- What sensations tell you that you are safe?
- What sensations tell you that you are not?
- When was the last time you checked in with your body before responding to the world?
- What might shift in your practice if you listened inward first?

Somatic Practice—The Listening Pause

- Take three slow breaths
- Inhale: notice where your body expands
- Exhale: notice where it contracts
- Name one area of openness and one area of guarding
- Ask that place gently: *What are you trying to tell me?*

Then—listen.

Closing Reflection

The body is not the problem
it is the portal.

Every ache, tremor, and sigh is an opening back to truth.

This is where the BYRD Model first takes root in the body
where theory becomes pulse,
and healing becomes a spiritual return.

The body, after all, is our first and last home.

Chapter 5
The Body and the System: How Racism Shapes Our Nervous Systems

(System Root Chapter—Systemic Racism
+ Your Testimony + Why BYRD Was Born)

Our bodies do not exist apart from systems—they live inside them.

Every racing heart, every clenched jaw, every exhaustion-soaked breath carries the imprint of the world we move through. When systems are oppressive, the body carries that oppression too. Systemic racism is not abstract. It is somatic.

This is the System Root—
the soil we grow in.

When the soil is toxic, the body adapts to survive.

The Roots Beneath Our Systems
Racism seeps into policies, institutions, and expectations—but it also seeps into our nervous systems. It shapes:

- how we breathe
- how we brace
- how we interpret danger

- how we navigate spaces not built for us

Until we name this soil, the branches of the mental health field cannot bear anything but the fruit of the systems that shaped them.

The History and Structure of Inequity

Systemic racism in mental health is neither an accident nor a recent phenomenon. Its roots run deep, entrenched in a history of medical exploitation and dehumanization. The mental health system was not designed for Black people or for BIPOC clinicians.

From medical experimentation documented in *Medical Apartheid*
to pseudoscience that framed Blackness as pathology
to cultural pathology theories that blamed communities for the harm systems created
the roots of this field are steeped in violence.

Even now, diversity language covers the structures of harm:

BIPOC clinicians are

- underadvanced

- overscrutinized

- excluded from decision-making

- burdened with the invisible tax of emotional labor

DEI is being dismantled nationwide, exposing how fragile progress has always been.

These inequities are visible everywhere: in the overrepresentation of BIPOC individuals in mental health diagnoses, the underrepresentation of BIPOC clinicians in leadership positions, and the lack of culturally responsive care. The architecture of our institutions still mirrors the biases of their creators.

As a Black clinician, I step into this field carrying intergenerational pain and wisdom—not just for myself, but for the countless BIPOC individuals who have navigated these systems before me. My multiple identities, as a Black woman, mother, healer, wife, and educator, place me at heightened risk of discrimination, erasure, and multifaceted harm. I exist at the intersection of mental health and social justice, and my personal and professional experiences have forced me to own my truth and actively participate in the change I seek. I can no longer wait on the sidelines for someone else to tap me into the game.

Why the BYRD Model Was Born

In the face of this deeply rooted inequity, I created the BYRD Model as a direct response to the harm embedded in these systems. It was born from the necessity of naming what traditional frameworks refuse to see, a pathway to healing that acknowledges the whole self: body, mind, and spirit. The model provides tools for transformation not only for the individual, but also for the larger systems that perpetuate harm. It offers a way to disrupt the very structures that have contributed to our collective trauma. I created the BYRD Model because traditional frameworks refuse to see what our bodies already know:

healing is not individual
healing is not raceless
healing is not separate from systems

The BYRD Model emerged as an act of resistance, a way to name injustice and reclaim the body as a site of liberation.

Personal Reflection

One of the most painful experiences of my career came when I created a wellness center for students at a local high school, a space designed to be a sanctuary where they could find peace, connection, and reflection during their breaks and lunches. This space quickly became a refuge, a place where students, particularly BIPOC students, felt seen, heard, and safe. I watched as the once-empty room came alive with laughter, stillness, and shared breath.

Then, just as quickly, it was taken away.
The principal, who had once shown no interest in the space, shut it down without warning or explanation. I saw the disappointment on the students' faces, their sense of safety ripped away with a single administrative decision. When I advocated for its reopening, I was met not with understanding, but with retaliation.

Suddenly, my every move was scrutinized. I was denied basic resources my colleagues received freely. I found myself isolated from my team, treated as if I had done something wrong when all I had done was create a space where Black and Brown students could breathe. The message was clear: spaces that bring joy and healing to BIPOC communities are seen as threats.

This experience is not unique to me—it is a reflection of a system that silences those who challenge it. It is the same system that tells Black clinicians to "just be grateful to be here" while denying us advancement. It is the same system that punishes those who speak up, who dare to demand better for themselves and their communities.

This is the invisible tax Black clinicians pay: the cost of advocating, the exhaustion of constantly fighting, the pain of watching systems prioritize control over care, suppression over healing, exclusion over equity.

But I refuse to be silent.
My story is one of many, but it is also a testament to resilience, advocacy,

and the unwavering belief that healing spaces belong to us.
No matter how many times they try to take them away, we will
build again.
We will carve out spaces for joy, for rest, for reflection, because our healing
is nonnegotiable.

Healing the healer means confronting not only our bodies, but the systems
that shaped their suffering. The work is not to choose between self-care
and systemic change; it is to understand that one cannot exist without
the other.

As we deepen into somatic work, we begin touching our Four Roots:
Identity, Story, Body, and System, each one whispering where healing is
asking to begin.

Healing the healer requires confronting both:

- the body

  and

- the systems that shaped its suffering

We do not get to choose between somatics and justice.
We need both.

As we deepen into our Four Roots, we begin to understand where healing
must begin and how far it must reach.

CHAPTER 6
HOW DISCRIMINATION AND BIAS MANIFEST IN CLINICAL INTERACTIONS

The Body Knows Before the Mind

Bias doesn't just happen in words, it happens in the body first. Our pulse quickens before the insult lands. Our shoulders rise before the dismissal is spoken. Our bodies know when we are being unseen. They register what our minds are sometimes too tired to name.

This is the cost of working within systems that mirror historical trauma: every microaggression becomes a small reenactment of erasure. And yet, we keep showing up—because healing is not only what we do; it's who we are.

Microaggressions and the Dismissal of Expertise

Bias in mental health settings is not always overt.
Often, it manifests as microaggressions—the subtle but insidious ways that competence is questioned, contributions are minimized, and expertise is dismissed based on race. These experiences are exhausting, disheartening, and unfortunately, all too common for Black clinicians.

Microaggressions slip quietly into professional spaces, shaping the air before we even speak. They create an environment where BIPOC clinicians are too often overlooked, dismissed, or treated as though our presence is incidental. I don't need a book to tell me this; I have lived it. I have felt the sting of being unseen and unheard in rooms where I was working twice as hard just to be recognized as worthy of being there. I've been in meetings where my ideas were dismissed, only to be restated by a white colleague minutes later and suddenly praised. I've watched promotions and leadership opportunities go to less experienced white clinicians while I was told to "be patient" or to "work on my approach." The underlying message was clear: I was expected to work twice as hard for half the recognition.

But what stings most is not just the dismissal of our expertise—it's the way we are expected to absorb it without complaint. We are asked to "rise above" the discrimination, to "not take it personally," to "focus on the work." But how do we focus when the work itself is laced with inequities? When the very spaces where we are supposed to help others continue to harm us?

Here, the BYRD Model becomes both mirror and medicine.
Through Belonging, I remind myself that my expertise is not up for debate, that I have earned my seat at the table. By asserting my contributions clearly and with confidence, I create safety for myself in spaces that would rather erase me.
Yielding invites me to notice when exhaustion begins to take root, to honor the body's signals instead of overriding them. Rest becomes strategy, not surrender.
Resilience connects me to a lineage of strength—reminding me that I stand on the shoulders of those who turned pain into purpose.
And Disruption empowers me to name inequity out loud, to challenge the system not from rage alone, but from love and integrity.

In this way, the BYRD Model doesn't just describe healing, it enacts it.

The Roots of Identity and Body
Each moment of bias strikes deeper than the mind—it lands in the body.
The tightening jaw, the shallow breath, the silent calculation of safety.
These reactions live in what I call our *Identity Roots* and *Body Roots.* Our identities—race, gender, class, faith—shape how we're seen and how we

see ourselves. Our bodies remember every moment we've had to defend that truth. When we begin to honor these roots, we start to see how our healing is not just about changing thoughts, but about tending to the ground beneath them.

Racialized Patient Dynamics

The weight of bias doesn't only come from colleagues or supervisors; it seeps into our work with patients as well.

I once had a patient who openly expressed racist beliefs in every session. With each encounter, I felt my nervous system brace itself, preparing to endure another round of harmful rhetoric disguised as "honest conversation."

At first, I believed professionalism would protect me. I told myself that my training could hold it all. But my body knew otherwise. My jaw clenched. My stomach tightened. My breath shortened. I was holding the weight of this patient's racism inside me—and it was taking a toll.

When I turned to my white supervisor for support, I expected empathy, validation, maybe even intervention. Instead, she said:

"You should feel honored that the patient feels comfortable enough to share."

Honored.

I was being asked to carry the burden of racism as part of my job description. To absorb harm quietly in the name of clinical neutrality. Once again, I was being told to silence my pain to protect someone else's comfort.

Here, the BYRD Model offers a lifeline.
Yielding allows me to acknowledge my distress and give myself permission to step back when necessary.
Resilience reminds me that this pain is not mine to internalize; it belongs to a system of harm, not my worth.

Disruption empowers me to set clear boundaries, to name the behavior directly, and to create space for accountability.

And Belonging reminds me that my well-being matters—that safety is not selfish; it's sacred.

Personal Reflection: Carrying the Weight into the Classroom

These same dynamics follow me into the classroom.

The microaggressions, the assumptions, the unspoken rules of who is allowed to lead, to challenge, to exist fully; they echo in academic spaces, too.

I remember teaching a *Cross-Cultural Counseling* course and encountering a student who challenged every word I spoke. It was relentless; each point I made, each example I gave, was met with skepticism or dismissal. I poured my energy into creating an engaging, meaningful class, but by semester's end, I was exhausted.

In the final class, three Latinx students spoke up. They turned to the room and said:

"Would this student be treating our professor this way if she were white?"

Their words hung in the air, heavy with truth.

It wasn't just one defiant student—it was a reflection of a system that conditions people to question, challenge, and undermine Black expertise. A system that whispers, *Prove yourself again. And again. And again.*

The reality is, I am not only preparing students to become therapists—I am preparing them to navigate a profession that was not built for all of them. I want to protect them from the harm I have endured, but what they need most is the truth. The truth about how racism shows up in clinical work. The truth about how their bodies will hold that weight. The truth that healing the system means first surviving it.

Healing is not only a personal journey. It is also shaped by the world around us. When we tend to our wounds, we are doing intimate inner work, and we are also participating in a much larger movement toward justice, dignity, and liberation, and so is teaching.
Every lecture, every story, every moment of truth-telling in my classroom is an act of resistance, a refusal to let silence win.

Closing Reflection

To be a Black clinician is to practice healing while standing inside the wound.
The work is to name it, to feel it, to transform it—and to remind ourselves that our presence in these spaces is not accidental. It is ancestral. It is necessary.

Through Belonging, Yielding, Resilience, and Disruption, we remember: our healing is not passive.
It is power.

CHAPTER 7
PERSONAL NARRATIVES OF NAVIGATING THE SYSTEM

A Childhood Shaped by Trauma and Resilience

My story begins in San Francisco, a city glittering with dreams and humming with danger. It was where my husband and I grew up, where we learned the unspoken rules of survival, where beauty and brutality lived side by side. The weight of survival was not a metaphor; it was a daily assignment.

One of the defining moments of my life came when I had to identify my cousin's body after he was shot. That moment carved itself into my soul. It wasn't only grief; it was a cellular shift—a lesson in how trauma etches itself into flesh, how it reorganizes the way we move through the world. I didn't have language for it then, but I could feel it pulsing beneath my skin.

As a survivor of sexual, physical, and emotional abuse, I know intimately that stress and trauma do not stay confined to the mind. They live in the body. They take up residence in muscle and marrow, shaping how we breathe, how we brace, how we expect the next blow even in moments of quiet. The ghosts of our past don't simply vanish; they echo through our nervous systems, unprocessed fragments trapped in time.

Trauma can be understood as an experience that overwhelms the body and mind before we have the capacity to make sense of it. It arrives with an intensity or speed that outpaces our ability to stay grounded, and it lingers without enough support or space to process what happened. That definition lives inside me. It is what it feels like to be a Black woman navigating a world that demands endurance but offers little repair. The nervous system does not forget. It holds every injustice, every betrayal, every unspoken grief, until one day the body can no longer bear the weight.

Somatic Pause

- Close your eyes. Let your shoulders fall.

- Notice one small place in your body that still feels like it's holding someone else's story.

- Exhale it, not to erase it, but to make room for your own.

Balancing the Roles of Clinician and Educator

My six daughters taught me stamina, tenderness, and systems-thinking, skills that no syllabus can confer. In the classroom, I see their resilience reflected in my students, especially first-gen and BIPOC students asked to prove themselves in spaces not built for them. I want to promise safety; instead, I promise truth, and tools.

Somatic Bridge

- Notice your seat. Feel the ground. Ask: *What does my body need to keep reading honestly?*

The Stroke That Changed Everything

November 18, 2024—my body decided what my mind kept postponing. Months of microaggressions, impossible workloads, and self-abandonment ended in collapse. In the ICU, the lie unraveled: I was pouring from a body I refused to protect. The body speaks with an honesty our minds sometimes avoid. It carries our history with perfect clarity and reveals what still needs tending. The body does not lie.

BYRD as Medicine

- Belonging: I return to myself. I stop earning visibility with overwork.

- Yielding: Rest becomes treatment, not guilt. I honor limits as sacred.

- Resilience: I rebuild around my well-being rather than around crisis.

- Disruption: I stop waiting for systems to shift; I change my participation in them.

Somatic Cue

One hand to heart, one to belly. *I choose to belong to myself.*

Closing Reflection

Bessel van der Kolk teaches that healing begins when we acknowledge trauma's impact on the body and restore balance. In the ICU I understood: I was not the only clinician suffering in silence. How many of us are walking the edge, ignoring the messages our bodies are screaming? I knew how I got there. I decided I wouldn't stay there.

This book is not only about harm; it is about the ways we heal. It is an invitation to step into our bodies, stories, truth. The BYRD Model is integral to this reclamation: Belonging creates spaces where we are fully seen; Yielding restores rest as medicine; Resilience reclaims our inherited strength; Disruption changes the systems that insist we disappear.

BYRD Call to Action

- Belonging: Begin meetings by naming your authorship when offering ideas. Track credit in writing.

- Yielding: Schedule recovery blocks like sessions—and protect them.

- Resilience: Create a "lineage list" of five people you call when breath gets small.

- Disruption: Convert patterns into policies (credit lines, meeting norms, escalation paths).

Part II:
The Significance of Embodiment and the Felt Sense of Discrimination

CHAPTER 8
EMBODIED TRAUMA—
THE BLACK BODY
CLINICIAN'S
EXPERIENCE

The Role of Intersectionality

Burnout is never just workload.
For Black women, it is the compounded cost of navigating institutions that were not built with us in mind.

Kimberlé Crenshaw reminds us that overlapping identities do not simply *add* pressure; they multiply it. In mental health settings, this looks like unequal pay, limited leadership opportunities, and constant scrutiny. It looks like being expected to mentor, soothe, and translate across cultures, often without compensation or acknowledgment.

Fariha Roisin asks, *"Who is wellness for?"*
And in our field, the answer is often: not the women of color doing the healing.

Somatic Bridge

Scan from scalp to soles.
Where does your body whisper, *"I'm doing too much"*?
Just notice. No fixing. Just presence.

Motherhood as a Professional Liability

My six daughters sharpened my clinical instincts long before any graduate program did. Motherhood taught me crisis assessment, patience, emotional attunement, and co-regulation. Yet in professional spaces, motherhood was framed as a liability rather than a strength.

When white peers spoke of their children, they were celebrated:
"Supermom!"
When I spoke of mine:
"How do you manage it all?"

The message was clear:
Care, when done by Black women, is seen as depletion—not leadership.

BYRD Reframe of Motherhood

- Belonging: I refuse to split myself. Motherhood and clinicianhood live in the same sacred body.

- Yielding: Recovery time is a requirement. Boundaries are clinical quality.

- Resilience: Motherhood is leadership—complex problem-solving under pressure.

- Disruption: I request structural support aligned with outcomes: equitable caseloads, schedule autonomy, and compensated mentorship.

Somatic Pause

- Inhale

- Hold

- Exhale

- Let the back of your heart soften.

The Exhausting Dance of Unseen Labor

Many Black clinicians know this dance:

- Leading, but not credited
- Being praised in private, erased in public
- Asked to solve problems we never created
- Expected to carry DEI on our backs
- Expected to say "yes" because we are "strong"

This is workload creep—the assumption that our competence is infinite and free.

Disruptive Asks (Clear and Concrete)

- Credit in agendas and postmortems
- Compensation for emotional labor and DEI work
- Transparent promotion rubrics
- Opt-out limits on extra tasks, not opt-in burdens

BYRD Lens Applied

- Belonging: Visibility is not vanity; it is safety.
- Yielding: "No" is a nervous-system boundary.
- Resilience: Joy replenishes capacity more than grit.
- Disruption: Align asks with metrics; accountability is kindness to the system and to the self.

Honoring Our Full Identities

Intersectionality means our struggles are interlocking, not isolated. Solutions cannot depend on individual self-care alone.

We require structural transformation:

- Compensation for emotional labor

- Promotion pathways that value cultural leadership

- Cultures where Black women's expertise is centered without tokenization

BYRD in Motion

- Belonging: Claim one space weekly where your full self is welcome.

- Yielding: Step back from rooms that drain your brilliance.

- Resilience: Shift from endurance to empowerment.

- Disruption: Redesign norms that keep erasing or minimizing your contributions.

Somatic Pause

- Feet flat.

- Press the ground.

- Feel the rise up your legs.

- Say aloud if you can:
  "I am not here to disappear."

Personal Reflection: A Season of Overextension

There was a time when sessions stacked without breath between them—trauma on top of trauma, hour after hour. Every request from leadership felt urgent; every "ask" felt nonnegotiable. What I truly needed was acknowledgment, sustainability, and support.

Instead, the message was:
"Just manage your time better."

But I wasn't asking for favors.
I was asking for humanity.

The headaches, the fatigue, the shallow breath—these were my body's early warnings. The truth was simple: I was internalizing systems that consumed my labor while denying my needs.

I realized that my healing could not depend on systems that benefited from my exhaustion.

The Awakening—BYRD as Self-Advocacy

1. Belonging:
   I belong in every room I serve, including the room of my own care.

2. Yielding:
   Rest is a clinical intervention. Limits are sacred data.

3. Resilience:
   Not the romance of endurance—intentional rebuilding rooted in dignity.

4. Disruption:
   I challenge roles that require my silence.
   I rewrite my participation contract.

A Call to Action

Self-advocacy is not indulgence.
It is survival.
It is strategy.
It is sacred.

We are not machines.
We are not infinite wells of emotional labor.
We are not required to set ourselves on fire to keep broken systems warm.

The BYRD Model guides the way:

- Belonging—Create spaces where your full self is not negotiable.
- Yielding—Put rest at the center of your clinical ethics.
- Resilience—Rebuild with intention, not obligation.
- Disruption—Demand accountability, dignity, and redesign at scale.

BYRD Call to Action

- Belonging: Choose one space per week where you feel fully seen—and schedule it.
- Yielding: Identify one role you will perform at 80 percent without apology.
- Resilience: Track one joy practice daily as if it were a vital sign.
- Disruption: Make one structural ask this quarter. Document it. Follow through.

CHAPTER 9
WHAT IT MEANS TO BE EMBODIED

$\mathcal{E}$mbodiment is more than inhabiting a body; it is the sacred act of returning home to it. It is listening to the whispers beneath the skin, honoring what tightens, what softens, what longs to rest. For Black clinicians, embodiment is both survival and rebellion.

Our bodies are archives, carrying personal memory, ancestral grief, and the hum of resistance. They hold both the ache and the art of living while Black in systems that demand our disconnection.

Kathy Kain, in *Nurturing Resilience*, reminds us that cultivating a *felt sense*, the ability to notice and respond to our body's cues, is critical for restoring balance after trauma. But oppression teaches us the opposite: to distrust our sensations, to override exhaustion, to tighten where we should release.

We are told to keep going. To look composed. To perform wellness even when our nervous systems are pleading for mercy.

Listening to My Body's Pleas

There was a time when my body was screaming for my attention, and I ignored it.

The signs began quietly: tightening chest, racing heart, shallow breath. My sympathetic nervous system, the gas pedal of survival, was jammed to the floor. Each morning, I woke already braced for microaggressions, dismissal, and the endless proving.

I kept going.
Because I had responsibilities.
Because I didn't want to be seen as weak.
Because stopping felt dangerous.

So my body found another way to reach me.
When I refused to slow down, it slammed on the brakes—dorsal vagal shutdown—the body's emergency exit. I felt myself slipping away, floating outside my own skin. I was exhausted but could not rest, numb but still expected to care for everyone else.

Peter Levine teaches that trauma does not live in the event, but in the body's response. My nervous system had been storing years of racialized tension, inequity, and survival stress, and it finally collapsed under the weight.

I understood this intellectually. I could diagram it, explain it to a class, treat it in others.
But embodiment is not a theory; it is a reckoning.

Somatic Bridge: The Pause Between Knowing and Being

- Close your eyes.

- Notice where your body is holding the workday.

- Is it in the jaw, the shoulders, the belly?

- Now whisper softly: *You don't have to hold it all tonight.*

The Challenge of Embodiment for Black Clinicians

For many Black clinicians, the body can feel like a battleground.
Resmaa Menakem writes that racial trauma lives in the body as chronic vigilance. We live half-braced, even in moments of quiet, because our nervous systems have learned that safety is conditional. Professional spaces often demand disembodiment. Productivity over presence. Politeness over truth.
We're told: push harder, stay late, be gracious, don't let them see

you sweat.

The result? We live split—mind performing competence, body bearing the cost.

But embodiment is where healing begins.

To heal is to trust the body again.

To listen before it screams.

To honor our needs with the same urgency we offer to others.

Embodiment is not indulgence; it is resistance.

It is not luxury—it is liberation.

A Path Back to the Body

My return was not cinematic. It began in whispers.

A sigh that finally escaped.

A moment where my breath deepened without permission.

A tear I didn't swallow back.

I began to notice:

the tightness in my chest,

the heaviness in my limbs,

the way my breath shortened near certain doorways.

Each cue was a message: *I'm still here. Please listen.*

The BYRD Model became my compass for this reclamation:

- Belonging—I learned that my body's signals were not interruptions but invitations. My tension was testimony. I began to believe my body deserved safety and space.

- Yielding—I stopped fighting the pause. I redefined rest as strength, not weakness. Yielding became sacred resistance.

- Resilience—I realized resilience was not stoicism. It was the alchemy of rebuilding gently after collapse.

- Disruption—I broke the silence. I stopped treating self-neglect as professionalism. I demanded care, starting with my own.

Somatic Reflection: The First Home

Hand on heart.
Whisper: *I belong here.*

Not in the system's image, but in my own skin.

Honoring My Body's Wisdom

For years I had treated rest like guilt.
Each boundary felt like betrayal.
But my body was never betraying me—it was trying to bring me home.

When I finally listened, I learned that healing begins with attention.
That saying "no" is not selfish; it's sacred.
That self-care is not self-centered; it's reparative justice.

Rest became reclamation.
Stillness became strategy.
Listening became love.

The Collective Journey of Embodiment

Our bodies are not only personal—they are communal.
When Black clinicians reclaim embodiment, we reclaim a lineage.
We interrupt the inherited belief that our labor is more valuable than our lives.

This act of returning to the body is not isolation, it's a gathering.
Each breath we reclaim creates ripples in our community, reminding others that rest is contagious, too.

Our ancestors endured disembodiment as survival; we practice embodiment as freedom.

This is collective medicine:
Grounding in presence.
Breathing through fear.
Claiming joy without apology.

Reclaiming Our Body's Power: The BYRD Model in Motion

1. Belonging—We belong to each other and to ourselves. Our presence in these rooms is not an exception—it is the restoration of balance.

2. Yielding—We yield to our truth. We listen to our limits before they become crises. Yielding is strategic softness.

3. Resilience—We redefine it not as relentless endurance but as graceful recovery.

4. Disruption—We challenge every system that tells us our exhaustion is noble. We build new ones where wellness is the metric of success.

A Reflection for You

If your body is tired, it's because it has worked miracles to keep you alive. If you feel numb, that too is intelligence, it's how your system bought you time.
Your body is not the problem; it's the poet, the prophet, the protector.

Take a moment.
Ask: *What is my body saying right now?*
Whatever it says, believe it.

You are not a machine. You are a miracle.
And miracles need maintenance.

Closing Reflection:
The Courage to Return to Ourselves

Embodiment is not easy. It is an act of defiance for bodies the world has taught to disappear.

Ken Hardy reminds us that racial trauma is cumulative—a lifetime of being unseen, misread, undervalued. But returning to ourselves is the revolution.

Our bodies are not burdens; they are blueprints.
Not weak; wise.
Not broken; sacred.

Healing begins not in the institution, but in the inhale.
The BYRD Model brings us back to the rhythm of our own humanity:
where Belonging grounds us,
Yielding restores us,
Resilience renews us,
and Disruption liberates us.

When we return to our bodies, we return to truth.
And that truth whispers:
You have always been whole.

Chapter 10
The Felt Sense of Discrimination

Discrimination is not just something we encounter.
It is something we carry.

It finds its way into the body without permission.
It lingers under the skin, tightening muscles, shortening breath, shifting posture, and building an invisible armor we never asked to wear.

It shows up in:

- the raised shoulders before we speak,
- the forced smile when we feel unseen,
- the exhaustion that sleep cannot touch.

Systemic oppression is not metaphorical:
it is physiological.
It embeds itself into our nervous systems, shaping how we brace, how we breathe, how we enter rooms where we know we will be read before we are heard.

For Black clinicians, and clinicians of color, this felt sense is not occasional.
It is a rhythm the body learns too well.

We walk into meetings with soft steps and braced hearts.
We hold our breath in hallways.
We tighten our stomachs before introductions.

The body becomes a ledger of every moment we had to shrink, smile, soothe, or survive.

The Burden of Authority: When the Body Anticipates Harm

In professional settings, discrimination does not simply hurt feelings it disrupts physiology.

For Black clinicians:

- rejection becomes muscle memory,

- vigilance becomes baseline,

- anticipation becomes posture.

We prepare for harm before it arrives.
We hold our breath entering spaces that were never built for us.
We scan for danger inside rooms labeled "clinical," "team," or "professional development."

The nervous system becomes a historian of inequity.

And the weight adds up.

The Weight of This Moment in America

This year has felt heavier in the body.

Across the nation, Black and Brown communities can feel the tremor again,
the sense that the ground is shifting beneath us.

Equity programs are being dismantled.
Policies meant to protect marginalized communities are being reversed.

Immigrant families are being shaken awake by raids.
Political leaders are caught sharing hateful messages and calling it humor.

Every headline, every rollback, every violation registers first in the nervous system:

a tightening of the chest,
a drop in the stomach,
a bracing behind the eyes.

Our bodies are always listening, even when we try not to.

Reclaiming the Body Through the BYRD Model

In a world that extracts so much from our bodies
our care, our labor, our compassion
the BYRD Model offers a different path.

Belonging

A reminder that we deserve to take up space without shrinking ourselves to fit systems too small.

Yielding

Rest as resistance.
Rest as reclamation.
Rest as returning home.

Resilience

Not endurance.
Not "powering through."
But rebuilding from a place of truth instead of trauma.

Disruption

Not destruction
but courage.
Naming what harms.
Refusing to normalize what breaks us.
Building new systems from the wisdom of embodied experience.

How My Own Body Carries It

I feel discrimination in my body before I can name it.

- My chest tightens when my expertise is dismissed.

- My stomach knots when a patient questions my competence.

- My legs grow heavy walking to my car after a day of "professionalism" that required hiding my humanity.

This is more than stress.
It is inherited survival.
It is learned vigilance.
It is the exhaustion of being hyper-visible yet unseen.

The BYRD Model teaches that naming the load is the first step in lifting it.

- Belonging: I am not the problem.

- Yielding: I can pause.

- Resilience: I can rebuild.

- Disruption: I will not quietly carry harm.

The Quiet Violence of Microaggressions

Sometimes it's not the overt harm that wounds deepest.
It's the tiny cuts delivered daily:

- A colleague brightens for others but goes flat when speaking to me.
- A patient requests a "second opinion" before I've even introduced myself.
- A supervisor claims "race doesn't matter in therapy."
- A coworker minimizes my distress to protect the system's image.

Each moment alone is small.
Together, they become thunder.

The shoulders rise.
The jaw tightens.
The breath shortens.

The body remembers what the room tries to deny.

Our Bodies Also Remember Strength

Our bodies are sites of wisdom, not just wounds.

They hold:

- the laughter that broke through the hardest days,
- the music that anchored us when nothing else could,
- the warmth of community that refused to let us fall apart.

When my chest tightens, I place my hand over my heart and breathe.
When my shoulders lift, I roll them back until they drop.
When my voice shakes, I hum until the vibration reminds me I am home inside myself.

These are not small acts.
They are quiet revolutions.

Healing in Community: Dr. Karen Roller's Wisdom

Healing has come to me through relationship
in conversations with other Black clinicians,
in the reflections of my daughters,
in the gentle truths shared by colleagues I trust.

Dr. Karen Roller once reminded me:

"Healing happens in relationship."

Not in isolation.
Not in silence.
Not in the systems that harm us.

But in the spaces where we are believed, seen, and held.

Her words stayed in my body as truth.
And they are part of the heartbeat of the BYRD Model.

Personal Reflection: When the Body Finally Spoke

I will never forget the moment my body told the truth louder than my mind.

A supervisor once questioned my understanding of patient care —
after asking me to rush trauma sessions to increase productivity.

As I walked to my car:

- my stomach twisted,
- my chest collapsed inward,
- my legs trembled.

My body was done protecting other people's comfort.
It was done absorbing harm to keep the peace.
It was done pretending to be fine.

That day my body said:
"No more."

And I listened.

Belonging reminded me I had the right to exist fully.
Yielding gave me permission to pause.
Resilience helped me turn pain into purpose.
Disruption helped me speak the truth—even when my voice quivered.

We are not only healers.
We are healing, too.

Closing Reflection: Honoring the Body's Truth

Racial trauma does not live in the past.
It lives in the body.

Healing begins the moment we stop running from ourselves.

Your body is not a burden.
It is a sacred archive of survival and possibility.

Ask yourself:

- Where does my body hold my story?
- What is it trying to tell me today?
- What would release feel like right now?

As you breathe into these questions, remember:

You are the proof of inherited resilience.
You are the bridge between what was broken and what is

becoming whole.
You are allowed to rest.
You are allowed to heal.
You are allowed to belong.

This is what it means to live the BYRD Model —
to Belong, Yield, Rise, and Disrupt.
To heal not just for survival, but for liberation.

Chapter 11
Foundations of Somatic Healing

"The body remembers the prayers they couldn't say aloud. And still—it rises."

Introduction: Returning to the Body

There is a moment, quiet, almost imperceptible, when the soul calls us home to the body.

It does not shout.

It hums.

It trembles softly beneath the skin, asking, *Can you still hear me?*

For so long, I mistook survival for living. I mistook movement for healing. I mistook silence for strength.

I ignored the whispers in my muscles, the tightening in my chest, the exhaustion that nested behind my eyes, because the world had taught me that rest was weakness and pain was proof of worth.

But the body never lies. It holds the story long after the mind tries to forget.

This is the sacred threshold where somatic healing begins.

It is not a return to comfort; it is a return to truth.

It is a reckoning with all that the body has held for generations: the grief, the vigilance, the strength, the songs.

For Black clinicians, this work is more than therapeutic; it is ancestral. We are tending to the bodies that carried fields, births, marches, and dreams.

We are mending the torn spaces between what we inherited and what we choose to become.

Somatic healing invites us to listen, not only to our breath and bones, but to the stories they carry.
It reminds us that our healing is not just our own. It belongs to the lineage of those who endured so that we could rest, those who prayed for a freedom they might never see, and those who still rise through us.

The chapters that follow are not instructions; they are invitations.
To pause.
To breathe.
To belong again to your body.

Because healing is not something we *do*, it's something we *remember*.
And every time we remember, we bring light to what has long
been silenced.
Every time we breathe deeply, we reclaim what was taken.
Every time we yield, we make space for joy to return.

So let us begin again, gently, honestly, wholly, with the truth that the body, too, deserves a voice.
And that voice has been waiting for you to listen.

Chapter 12
What Is Somatic Healing?

Opening Reflection

Healing is often framed as a cognitive process, shifting thoughts, increasing awareness, resolving conflicts. But true healing is not just intellectual; it is embodied. It moves through the nervous system, the breath, the muscles, and the spirit.

For Black clinicians and POC, somatic healing is more than tending our own wounds—it is honoring the imprints of our lineage. Our bodies hold the wisdom of survival, resistance, and transformation. We carry living archives inside of us: echoes of vigilance, echoes of prayer, echoes of endurance.

The stress responses we feel today are not simply "symptoms." They are somatic memories shaped across centuries, written into our physiology by injustice, yet held together by our ancestors' resilience.

Somatic healing becomes an act of reclamation. A way to honor what was endured and reclaim what was denied: ease, breath, rest, and joy. It reminds us that healing is both personal and communal, woven through lineage, belonging, and liberation.

Understanding Somatic Healing

At its essence, somatic healing is a return to the body—listening to its signals, feeling its truths, and transforming the patterns it holds. Trauma is not only a memory; it is an embodied experience. Even when the mind "understands," the body may still brace.

For Black clinicians, racialized stress shows up somatically:
the chest tightening when we're dismissed,
the jaw clenching when competence is doubted,
the heaviness that follows a microaggression.

These sensations are not signs of weakness; they're imprints of survival.

Somatic healing teaches us to notice these signals with care, to interrupt old patterns, and to build new pathways of safety. It is not indulgence. It is resistance. It is reclaiming joy in a body the world tried to harden.

Somatic Experiencing and the BYRD Model:
A Holistic Pathway

Somatic Experiencing (SE) reconnects us to the body's brilliance—its capacity to release trapped energy, to pendulate from activation to ease, to return to balance.

The BYRD Model: Belonging, Yielding, Resilience, and Disruption creates a cultural and emotional foundation beneath that physiological work:

- Belonging roots us in safety.

- Yielding teaches us that rest is sacred.

- Resilience reminds us that strength is inherited.

- Disruption challenges the systems that harmed us.

SE works inside the nervous system.

The BYRD Model works inside the story.
Together, they create a map from survival to sovereignty.

Healing becomes not about "fixing" the body but learning its language—curiosity over judgment, presence over performance.

Honoring Ancestral Wisdom

Our ancestors survived by listening to their bodies, through grief, through brutality, through creation. Their strength was somatic. Their faith was somatic. Their joy was somatic.

We inherit both wounds and wisdom.

Somatic healing awakens the embodied resilience they passed down: the rhythm, the grounding, the knowing that lived beneath oppression. When we heal, we do not heal alone—we heal in a lineage. We return strength to those who prayed for it. We free future generations to feel differently inside their bodies.

Introducing the Four Roots Framework

To deepen and ground the BYRD Model, I developed the Four Roots Framework—a way to understand how healing is shaped not just by experience, but by identity, memory, embodiment, and system.

These are the roots beneath our healing:

1. Identity Roots

Our social and cultural identities—race, gender, class, sexuality, ability, faith, migration—shape our access to safety and belonging. Healing requires naming how these identities impact our nervous system and our visibility.

2. Story Roots

The narratives we inherit—family patterns, cultural myths, ancestral lessons, media messages—inform our meaning-making. Healing lets us re-author those stories: keeping what nourishes us and composting what harms us.

3. Body Roots

Our nervous system imprints: fight, flight, freeze. Trauma and safety shape these patterns. Healing begins with awareness and grows through choice.

4. System Roots

Structures and institutions, healthcare, education, and workplace culture shape which bodies are protected and which are pathologized. Healing here means personal liberation *and* systemic change.

These Roots create the soil where the BYRD Model grows.
They anchor the work in lineage, body, and justice.

Bridging Ancestral Knowledge and Somatic Practice

Our ancestors' wisdom hums beneath our skin. SE gives us tools to hear that hum. It turns inherited vigilance into embodied freedom.

When the breath catches, when the shoulders rise, when the heart races—these aren't flaws. They are messages. SE teaches us to interpret them, not fear them. To shift from reactivity to regulation. To transform the echo of generational survival into present-day safety.

Somatic Experiencing and Racial Trauma

Racial trauma lodges in the body. It keeps us braced, scanning, preparing. SE meets this reality with gentleness, through titration, pendulation, and co-regulation. It invites us to release stress at a pace that honors the body's timing.

For Black clinicians and POC, regulating our own systems is a quiet revolution.
Every breath of ease is a refusal to carry the weight alone.
Every release is a return to dignity.

The Body as Sanctuary

Somatic healing is about reclaiming the body as home. A place of rest, not performance. A place of joy, not tension. Through grounding, breathwork, and mindful awareness, we build a new relationship with ourselves—one rooted in trust.

Our bodies are always speaking. Always guiding. Always seeking balance.

Healing becomes a conversation:
"I'm listening."
"I hear you."
"I'm with you."

Closing Reflection

Healing is not a destination. It is a return, a remembering of the body's power and the lineage it carries.

We are healers who hold others while holding ourselves. We are descendants of endurance and ancestors of possibility. Our bodies are not just vessels; they are sanctuaries, archives, and altars.

May you listen to your body's whispers.
May you trust its timing.
May you honor its wisdom.

Because the body does not lie.
And when you listen... it tells you how to rise.

Somatic Practice Reflection Box: Coming Home to the Body

Grounded Belonging

- Feet on the floor

- Press gently downward

- Whisper: *I belong here. My body belongs here.*

Yielding Breath

- One hand on chest, one on belly

- Inhale, exhale

- Release one thing your body no longer needs

Resilient Recall

- Call in an ancestor

- Notice where you feel them

- Let their strength settle into your bones

Gentle Disruption

- When tension speaks, pause

- Name it: *"My body is asking to be heard."*

- Offer care: a boundary, a stretch, a sip of water, a breath

Closing Reflection

"My body is not my enemy. It is my guide. I am learning to listen, to yield, and to heal."

Chapter 13
Somatic Approaches in Mental Health

Healing Through the Body

Healing trauma is not about erasing what happened; it is about understanding how our bodies have carried it.
It is a homecoming. A slow, sacred remembering.

Trauma is not just a story we tell in therapy rooms; it is an imprint, a trembling in the nervous system, a tightening in the chest, a shallow breath that forgets how to expand. It shapes how we move through the world, how we love, how we rest, and how we survive.

Somatic approaches honor this truth. They bridge the wisdom of the body with the insight of the mind, offering pathways to healing that are not about fixing, but about *feeling*, about reclaiming what has always belonged to us.

My journey into somatic healing began when my body stopped whispering and started screaming. For years, I had pushed through exhaustion, microaggressions, and the relentless pressure of caregiving in systems not built for my well-being. My body carried it all until it couldn't.

And then came my stroke.
The ICU was quiet except for the hum of machines, a sterile kind of stillness that made every thought louder. I lay there, disconnected from my right leg, wondering if I would ever walk again. My body felt foreign, like a place I no longer knew how to inhabit.

Tommy stood beside me, unwavering. When I asked, through tears, *"What is going to happen to me?"* he said, "Speak your faith and your wishes for healing out loud. Your body will listen."

So I did. Hesitant, trembling, but determined.
I spoke to my body like it was someone I loved:
"Leg, move. Body, heal."

At first, there was nothing. Then, a flicker, a small shift, like my body was remembering me. That was the moment I understood: healing isn't about force; it's about invitation. The body doesn't respond to command; it responds to compassion.

That moment taught me what every somatic practice is built upon: that the body will listen when it finally feels safe enough to speak.

Somatic Experiencing (SE)

Somatic Experiencing (SE), developed by Peter Levine, is a practice of listening to the body's unfinished stories. Trauma isn't in the event itself— it's in the body's response, in the energy that never got to move, in the survival impulse that never found rest.

SE teaches us to slow down, to notice the micro-movements, the sensations, the breath, the tremble, all the subtle signs that the body is doing its sacred work of recalibration.

I remember one of my first SE sessions. My practitioner asked me to track the sensation in my chest, the familiar tightness that had followed me for years. As I stayed with it, breathing, not fixing, I felt an old memory rise: a meeting where I was dismissed, my words drowned out by someone who didn't see me. My body had been holding that moment, quietly, faithfully.

When I finally allowed it space to move, to breathe, to release, the tension softened. My chest opened. My body let out a sigh I didn't know it was holding. It wasn't just relief; it was liberation.

This is what SE offers: a return to the body's own language. A reminder that every ache has meaning. Every tremor has truth. Every stillness holds wisdom.

Sensorimotor Psychotherapy

Sensorimotor Psychotherapy brings mindfulness to the body's patterns, the posture, the breath, the small movements that tell the story before words ever arrive. It invites us to notice how emotion lives in muscle and bone.

For me, this work illuminated the unspoken patterns I carried from childhood, the instinct to shrink when conflict arose, the way my shoulders tightened when I felt unseen. My body had learned these postures as protection. Through gentle awareness, I began to unlearn them.

This process is not about control; it's about curiosity.
What does my body do when I feel unsafe?
Where does my breath go when I'm afraid to speak?
What happens when I allow myself to stay with the discomfort instead of escaping it?

Sensorimotor work taught me to bring compassion to my body's defenses, to thank them for helping me survive. And in that gratitude, the healing began.

Yoga and Breathwork

There are moments in recovery when the body feels like foreign soil. After my stroke, even lifting my leg felt like climbing a mountain. The fear of failing my own body was heavy, heavier than the weakness itself.

A trauma-informed yoga teacher helped me begin again, slowly and reverently. Gentle stretches. Breath that met me where I was. No pressure, no push, only presence.

I found comfort in the quiet rhythm of Soul Haum @ Home, led by

Jasmine Allen, a space that blended yoga, Somatic Experiencing, and spirit. Through her guidance, I learned to approach my body not as something broken, but as something brave.

Some days, the work was nothing more than breath, steady and intentional. Other days, movement returned like grace, soft and surprising. Every inhale became a prayer. Every exhale, a release.

Breathwork grounded me when my mind spiraled into fear. Not through control or counting, but through trust, the kind that says, *You are safe to breathe again.*

Yoga and breathwork became less about physical rehabilitation and more about reuniting with myself. They reminded me that even after trauma, the body still longs for wholeness. And when we listen gently enough, it shows us the way home.

Polyvagal Practices

The vagus nerve—that long, wandering messenger between body and brain—is the quiet architect of our sense of safety.
Through Stephen Porges' Polyvagal Theory, we learn that connection itself is medicine. When the body feels safe, the nervous system begins to harmonize.

For me, healing came through small, holy rituals: humming softly while cooking, singing in the shower, placing a hand over my heart and whispering, *I'm here.*
Each act was a signal to my nervous system, a love letter to my own biology.

These gestures, though simple, reminded me that healing does not always come from grand breakthroughs. Sometimes it comes from a vibration, a breath, a moment of stillness that says, *You are no longer in danger.*

Polyvagal work invites us to tune our nervous systems toward connection, toward belonging, toward grace.

Healing as Resistance

Somatic work is not just therapy; it is rebellion.

In a world that profits from our exhaustion, choosing to rest is revolutionary.

In systems that try to dictate our worth, reclaiming our bodies is an act of defiance.

For Black clinicians, embodiment is protest. It says, *I will not numb myself for your comfort. I will not shrink to fit your safety. I will feel. I will rest. I will heal.*

Healing is resistance because it disrupts the legacy of harm. It interrupts the lie that our bodies exist only for labor, not for love. It reminds us that liberation is not only fought for, it is *felt.*

If you ever feel disconnected or overwhelmed, start small.

Place a hand on your chest.

Breathe in.

Let your body know that you are listening.

You are not broken. You are sacred.

Closing Reflection

Every body tells a story, not in words, but in rhythm.

The body remembers what the mind forgets, but it also remembers how to rise.

These somatic approaches, from SE to breathwork, are not steps to mastery but invitations to intimacy. They teach us to move from judgment to curiosity, from disconnection to belonging.

Healing is not a return to who we were before the pain. It is the sacred becoming of who we are after it.

So breathe. Tremble. Rest.
Let your body show you the way home.

Because within you, beneath the scars, beyond the survival
there is a pulse that hums,
I am still here.
And that pulse, that quiet rhythm of resilience,
is the sound of your freedom.

Reflection & Practice:
Coming Home to the Body

Healing through the body is not a linear journey; it is a rhythm.
It requires gentleness, curiosity, and the willingness to listen to the smallest whispers of truth.
These reflections and practices invite you to slow down and begin again, right where you are.

Reflection Prompts

1. The Whisper and the Shout

    - Where in your body do you feel the whispers, the quiet signals asking for your attention?

    - Where do you feel the shouts, the tension, the ache, or the fatigue that demands to be heard?

    - What might your body be trying to communicate that your mind has been too busy to hear?

2. Inherited Strengths

    - When you think of your ancestors—those who survived,

created, and loved before you—what embodied wisdom might you have inherited from them?

- How does your body carry its resilience? Its prayers? Its unfinished songs?

3. The Cost of Resilience

- What does "resilience" feel like in your body, not as a concept, but as a sensation?

- Where does it feel heavy?

- What might it look like to transform resilience into rest, softness, or joy?

4. Healing as Belonging

- When do you feel most at home in your body?

- What moments, spaces, or relationships allow you to exhale fully, without performance, without defense?

- What would it mean to belong to your body as deeply as you belong to your purpose?

Somatic Practices

Each of these can be done in under five minutes.
Start slow. Let your body guide the pace.
Remember: *healing happens when safety and curiosity meet.*

1. The Ground Beneath You

- Sit or stand with your feet flat on the floor.

- Notice the ground supporting you. Feel its steadiness.

- Gently rock your weight from side to side, front to back, sensing stability beneath movement.

- Whisper to yourself:
I am supported. I am allowed to be here.

This practice activates Belonging, reminding your nervous system that you are safe to take up space.

2. The Yielding Breath

- Place one hand on your heart, one on your lower belly.

- Inhale slowly through your nose for a count of four.

- Exhale through your mouth for a count of six.

- Feel your shoulders drop as you breathe out.

- Repeat five times, whispering with each exhale:
  I release what is not mine to carry.

This practice cultivates Yielding, the sacred rest that says, "I do not have to hold it all."

3. The Ancestral Pulse

- Close your eyes. Imagine the faces, hands, and songs of those who came before you.

- Feel their breath move through yours, their rhythm pulsing in your heartbeat.

- Gently sway your body as if rocked by their memory.

- Say softly:
  "I am the continuation of those who survived. My healing honors them."

This awakens Resilience, the strength that comes from remembering we do not heal alone.

4. The Disruption Shake

- Stand tall. Loosen your jaw, your shoulders, your knees.

- Begin to shake—your hands, your arms, your whole body.

- Let sound move through you, a sigh, a hum, a moan, a laugh.

- Keep shaking until you feel energy shift.
- When you stop, pause. Breathe.
- Feel what is different.

This practice embodies Disruption, shaking free the systems that have settled into our bones.

Closing Ritual: Coming Home

When you are ready, place your hand over your heart and whisper to yourself:

I am not broken.
I am becoming.
My body is both the question and the answer.

Take one more breath.
Feel the quiet hum inside you.
That is your wholeness
not waiting to be found,
but already here.

CHAPTER 14
THE FOUR ROOTS IN THE LIVING BODY

*H*ealing does not end with understanding the body. It begins when that understanding is lived.

By the time my body faced the uncertainty of a breast cancer scare, I already knew the language of somatic healing. I understood sensation. I respected nervous system pacing. And still—when the mass was found—my body responded before thought could catch up.

My breath shortened.
My ribs tightened.
My pelvis braced as if preparing to absorb impact.

This was not ignorance.
This was inheritance.

The body does not forget what the lineage learned to survive.

What followed was not a return to technique, but a return to **Roots**.

Belonging—Staying Inside the Body

Belonging, in that season, meant refusing to abandon myself.

In exam rooms and waiting rooms, wrapped in thin paper gowns, I practiced staying. One hand on my sternum. One hand resting low, where fear had settled. I did not rush reassurance. I did not demand calm.

I simply stayed.

Belonging is not comfort.
It is presence without betrayal.

For bodies shaped by racism, medical mistrust, and historical neglect, belonging begins when we stop forcing strength and allow the body to take up space as it is.

Yielding—Letting the Body Lead

Yielding came at night.

That was when my body finally released what I had been holding the way Black women are taught to hold everything—silently, efficiently, alone.

The trembling came first.
Then the ache.
Then the deep, unfamiliar permission to soften.

Yielding is not giving up.
It is letting the body set the pace instead of the mind.

In that yielding, my body taught me something no technique ever could: rest is not collapse when it is chosen.

Resilience—What We Inherit, Not What We Prove

Resilience did not show up as strength.

It showed up as memory.

As I lay still, I felt the echo of women before me—aunties, grandmothers, ancestors who carried fear in silence and learned to keep going anyway. Their endurance lived in my tissues. Their vigilance lived in my breath.

But resilience is not just what we carry forward.
It is also what we decide to transform.

Every time I chose softness instead of bracing, my body sent a different message down the lineage:

You will not inherit my exhaustion.
You will inherit my care.

That is epigenetic healing.

Disruption—Refusing to Heal Quietly

Disruption arrived quietly, not as rage, but as refusal.

I refused to rush my body back into productivity.
I refused to minimize fear in the name of professionalism.
I refused to treat my body as collateral damage for survival.

For healers of color, disruption often looks small from the outside—a boundary, a pause, a no spoken without apology.

But the body knows the truth.

Disruption is liberation practiced at the cellular level.

Healing That Moves Forward

This is where healing turns outward.

The Four Roots are not just personal practices; they are **ways of living** that ripple into our work, our families, our students, and the systems we touch.

Belonging changes how we show up.
Yielding changes how we pace care.
Resilience changes what we pass down.
Disruption changes what we refuse to normalize.

Healing does not ask us to return to who we were before harm.
It asks us to live differently because we listened.

Reflection & Practice: Living the Roots

Belonging

Where does your body ask you to stay instead of perform?

Yielding

What effort could soften if you trusted your body's timing?

Resilience

What strength did you inherit—and what burden are you ready
to release?

Disruption

What pattern no longer deserves your endurance?

Closing Threshold

Place one hand on your heart.
Let the other rest where your body feels most honest.

Whisper to yourself:

I am not broken.
I am becoming.
My body remembers how to lead me forward.

This is not the end of healing.
It is the moment healing learns how to walk with you.

Chapter 15
Somatic Abolitionism—Origins, Four Roots & Practice

$\mathcal{S}$omatic abolitionism teaches us something simple and profound: oppression is not just social or historical, it is somatic.
Bodies hold the bracing, the shrinking, the fawning, the silence.
Bodies also hold the possibility of release, expansiveness, clarity, and collective repair.

Liberation must be embodied because harm has been embodied.
This work unfolds through the nervous system, through relationship, and through structures—all three braided together.

And as we explored in the Four Roots Framework earlier in this book, liberation takes shape across identity, story, body, and systems.
Somatic abolitionism simply asks us to bring all four into the room at once, gently, honestly, and with reverence.

Somatic Abolitionism as Embodied Liberation

Instead of intellectualizing supremacy culture, we feel where it lives:

- the jaw that clamps when our brilliance is doubted,

- the breath that shortens in the presence of authority,

- the spine that curls inward to avoid being seen too fully,

- the micro-freezes that come after microaggressions.

Somatic abolitionism is the practice of unbracing.
Unlearning what the body had to do to survive.
Remembering what the body can do when it feels safe enough to choose something new.

It is not metaphor.
It is muscle.
It is memory.
It is the body moving from inherited fear into embodied freedom.

Core Principles

1. Name the Wound

As we've already grounded ourselves in earlier chapters: identity, story, body, and systems all shape how trauma settles into us.
Naming is the first interruption.

"This tightness makes sense."
"This shutdown has a history."
"There is nothing wrong with me, something happened to me and around me."

Naming shifts the story.
It unwinds the shame.

2. Begin in the Body

Liberation begins in sensation.

A warm hand to the heart.
Feet remembering the ground.
A slow orienting of the eyes around the room.

Not to erase pain—but to make room for choice.

Safety is not an idea.
It is a felt experience.

3. Root in Ancestry & Narrative

We inherit both trauma and genius.

Calling in ancestors—through breath, song, memory, language—expands
our capacity.
It reminds the nervous system:

"I am not the first.
I am not alone.
I come from people who have survived harder things than this."

Our stories reorganize the moment we author them with truth.

4. Repair Through Community & Structure

Regulation is relational.

A co-regulating presence.
An affinity space that centers truth.
A supervisor who names what others avoid.
Policies that protect instead of punish.

When institutions repair, bodies repair.
When systems soften, breath deepens.

Liberation is both internal and infrastructural.

A Clinician's Vignette (Atlanta, SEP Cohort)

I entered a BIPOC-only demo believing I would work through an old childhood story—something tidy, something familiar. But the body rarely follows the mind's agenda.

My faculty lead, Dea Parsanishi, stood before us, grounded as a mountain. She held the room with a presence that felt like ceremony. Her voice, steady, unhurried, and rooted in reverence, invited me to listen to what my body wanted to bring forward, not what my mind wanted to control. As I began to settle into the chair, I felt a stirring deep in my chest, a pressure that refused to quiet itself. Dea noticed the subtle shift in my breath and gently asked, "What's happening in your body right now?"

Her question opened a door. I closed my eyes and, instead of returning to childhood, I was suddenly with my cousin—the one whose death I had carried in silence. The grief rose, uninvited but insistent, pulsing through my ribs like an echo I had been too afraid to hear. I hadn't planned to speak his name that day, but my body decided it was time.

The room, full of Black, Indigenous, and Brown clinicians, became a sacred container. I could feel their presence wrapping around me like a prayer. No one rushed me. No one pathologized the tears that trembled just beneath my skin. I called my cousin's memory in, not as ache, but as anchor. His love, his laughter, his humanity, they all arrived, surrounding me in warmth.

Dea guided me to track my movements. "Stay with the movement," she said gently.
"Let your body complete what it never got to finish."

And it did.

A shake.
A shiver.
A softness.

Weight moved from my chest into my feet.
My breath widened.

My cousin's love rose through me, not as ache, but as anchor.

Identity honored.
Story reclaimed.
Body reorganized.
System (the room itself) became sanctuary.

I felt the weight shift from my chest into my feet. A slow exhale found me, as if my nervous system had been waiting years for that release. My breath widened. My back lifted. My eyes opened to the faces of my cohort, witnesses, healers, kin, each one holding space for my reclamation. Dozens of nervous systems co-regulating in liberation.

In that moment, identity was honored. Story was rewritten. Body was softened. And because the room was designed for us, for our colors, our rhythms, our truths, the system itself became a site of repair. When I finally stood, the room was quiet except for the sound of breathing, dozens of nervous systems co-regulating in shared liberation. My body knew where to go when I let it lead.

Lessons from Dea: The Power of Embodied Witnessing

That day with Dea taught me something no textbook ever could—that healing is not born from expertise alone, but from *presence*. She didn't rush to interpret or analyze; she created space wide enough for my nervous system to unfold at its own pace. Her silence was not absence, it was sacred accompaniment.

When she said, *"Let your body complete what it never got to finish,"* she wasn't asking me to be brave. She was inviting my body to be *free*.

Dea modeled the kind of practitioner I aspire to be, one who knows when to guide and when to get out of the way. She showed me that cultural attunement is more than awareness, it's embodiment. It's the ability to sense when a nervous system needs space, when silence is medicine, and when collective breath can do what words cannot.

Dea taught me what a regulated, abolitionist presence feels like:

- She did not manage me.

- She did not analyze me.

- She *accompanied* me.

Her stillness was medicine.
Her attunement was advocacy.
Her silence was protection.

This is somatic abolitionism in action:

- Identity honored through culturally safe space

- Story reshaped through truthful witnessing

- Body reorganized through safety

- System repaired through intentional design

Byrd Roots

- Identity Roots are honored when a space is built for our lived realities, not around them.

- Story Roots shift when we're invited to tell the truth of our pain and our power.

- Body Roots reorganize when safety is present and witnessed.

- System Roots begin to heal when institutions make room for this kind of presence.

Dea taught through being. She reminded me that true healing is communal, a choreography of breath, trust, and belonging. When I walked out of that room, I didn't just leave lighter, I left more whole. My cousin's love lived in me differently, and so did my own.

And that day, it led me home.

Instructor Reflection:
Facilitating Embodied Witnessing

Dea's guidance that day became a living lesson in what it means to facilitate *healing through presence*. As clinicians and educators, our work is not to fix or interpret, it is to create the conditions where the body can remember safety.

Embodied witnessing begins long before the session or classroom. It starts with our own regulation. Before we can hold space for another person's nervous system, we must anchor in our own. Breath first. Feet grounded. Shoulders soft. Only then can we model what it feels like to be with intensity without becoming consumed by it.

1. Regulate before you lead.
Your nervous system is the first co-regulator in the room. If you enter dysregulated, the space will mirror it. A simple grounding cue, one hand on the heart, one on the belly, reminds both you and your clients that calm is possible.

2. Honor the body's pace.
Trauma moves on its own timeline. Dea's question, *"What's happening in your body right now?"* wasn't a push—it was an invitation. Clinicians must learn to listen for the nervous system's consent. When the body says "pause," we pause. That's where trust is built.

3. Witness without agenda.
Embodied witnessing is not passive; it's intentional presence. It says, *I see you. I'm here. I won't look away.* It asks nothing of the other person

except truth. Sometimes the most profound intervention is a quiet, attuned silence.

4. Hold all Four Roots at once.
Healing deepens when we recognize what's at play beyond the individual body. Not by teaching them, but by *attuning through them*.

- Identity Roots: Whose body is in the room, and how has it been treated historically?

- Story Roots: What narratives shape this moment of pain or possibility?

- Body Roots: What sensations or impulses want to be acknowledged?

- System Roots: What external forces have influenced this nervous system's sense of safety?

When all four roots are held, witnessing becomes liberation—not just therapy.

5. End with ritual, not summary.
After deep somatic work, don't rush to summarize. Invite breath. Invite grounding. Invite gratitude. Ritual honors the sacredness of what has been shared and signals to the body that the moment of intensity is complete.

Somatic Practices

A. Naming Protocol—2–3 minutes

Roots: Identity • Story • Body

- Find one sensation. Label it (tight/buzzy/dull/hot).

- Add context: *This response makes sense given who I am and where I am.*

- Give it room: *This belongs for now. I don't have to fix it.*

- Track micro-changes (location, size, temperature).

B. Grounding Trio—60–90 seconds each

Roots: Body

- Feet remembering gravity

- Hand at heart

- Soft orienting of gaze
  Body Roots settle when given support.

C. Ancestral Invocation—1–2 minutes

Roots: Story • Identity
Call in someone whose breath made yours possible. Ask for steadiness, courage, or clarity. Listen with your body for the answer (breath drop, warmth, softening, tingling).

Feel the shift.

D. Boundary Rehearsal—2 minutes

Roots: Body • System
Stand. Feel your feet. Say twice, out loud:
"I'm not available for that. Here's what I can offer instead."
Notice sensations before/after. You are installing a boundary into muscle memory.

E. Collective Regulation—5 minutes in groups

Roots: System

- 60 seconds of shared silence.

- One person names a sensation; the group breathes with them.

- Rotate. No fixing. Only witness, breath, presence. A micro-model of cultural repair.

A Word to Institutions (System Roots)

If you lead people, you steward nervous systems. Build embodied equity into operations:

- Protected affinity/process spaces on the calendar.

- Trained, accountable supervision that names race, culture, and community as central to care.

- Clear, enforced anti-harassment pathways with somatic aftercare (not just paperwork).

- Workload and pay aligned with emotional labor. Accountability is not punishment; it is a regulation event for the whole system. It lowers the heart rate of the whole system.

Sacred Allyship

When allies move beyond statements into embodied support, steady presence, reparative action, resources that matter—Black bodies and POC receive a counter-message: *Your wholeness is nonnegotiable here.* That message settles shoulders and lengthens breath. Rewires culture. That is abolitionism in the body.

Reflection & Practice—A Four Roots Review Without Repetition

- Identity: What identity needs more spaciousness this week?

- Story: What narrative are you retiring? What replaces it?

- Body: One minute of breath with softened shoulders.

- System: One small repair you will move toward.

Closing Reflection

Hand at heart.
Hand at belly.

I am sacred body.
I am allowed to rest.
I am allowed to rise.
I am allowed to be free.

Chapter 16
The Intergenerational Wisdom of Healing

We inherit more than pain.

We inherit brilliance, ingenuity, humor, rhythm, and the quiet ways our people have always made life possible. Our ancestors didn't just endure—they innovated, resisted, loved, created, and carved out joy under impossible conditions. That endurance is in us. It's braided into our rituals, stitched into our laughter, and alive in the ways we reach for one another when life gets heavy.

I feel that lineage in small, everyday ways:

— In my mother's laughter, deep, full, and unapologetic, a sound that dared the world to dim her light.
— In the songs she hummed while cooking, melodies carried from her mother's kitchen to mine.
— In the way my parents taught perseverance and pride without ever needing to put it into words.
— In the instinct that makes me reach for my daughters' hands the same way my mother reached for mine.

These moments remind me: my body is not only where pain lives—it's where joy, strength, belonging, and transformation live too. Intergenerational healing isn't just about tending to wounds. It's about reclaiming the wisdom and resilience that were handed down alongside them.

Our healing is our inheritance.
Our joy is our birthright.
Our wisdom is timeless.

Collective Healing as Liberation

Reconnecting with the body is not a solo act—it is a collective practice of remembering. Healing happens in the presence of people who truly see us, hold us, and affirm our worth. For BIPOC clinicians, this truth is essential. Too many of us have been taught to endure alone, to push through when our bodies are pleading for rest.

I think of Karen offering energy medicine after my stroke, her quiet, grounded presence honoring that healing lives in emotional, spiritual, and ancestral layers, not just the physical. I think of hands laid on me in church, prayers whispered on my behalf, elders whose guidance steadied my steps. Community has held me when I was too tired to hold myself.

And I think of when community felt fractured, when scarcity, competition, or unhealed pain spoke louder than love. Months after my stroke, I reached out for connection and was met with conditions: support only if I could provide something in return. That moment didn't just sting; it revealed what oppression teaches us: to ration compassion and treat help like currency.

Resilience isn't the erasure of pain; it's the capacity to hold pain with support. But when the people around us are carrying their own unresolved burdens, our collective capacity thins.

This is why community care is liberation:
When we heal together, we break the isolation oppression depends on.

Remember:

- You do not have to heal alone.

- Your healing is not transactional.
- Your worth is not contingent on what you produce.

Healing in connection is healing in freedom.

A Vision for Sacred Healing

Our bodies are sacred repositories of both struggle and triumph. They remember the grief we swallowed, the harms we endured, and the ways we twisted ourselves to fit into spaces never built for us. They also remember dance, laughter, praise, deep rest, and the sweet exhale of being witnessed without judgment.

Somatic abolitionism calls us to honor this duality, to treat the body not as a battleground but as a sanctuary.

For me, this has meant releasing what no longer serves:

- the old scripts of unworthiness,
- the demand to endure without rest,
- the shame of needing help,
- the belief that acceptance must be earned through disappearance.

After my stroke, I saw something clearly: not everyone is meant to walk every mile with me. Expecting others to be what they cannot be is not fairness; it is self-abandonment. So I turned inward:

- What do I expect of myself?
- How can I cultivate safety inside my own body?
- What does it mean to honor my needs without apology?

I am writing a new story, one that centers my body as sacred ground. My healing is not something I earn. It's something I claim.

When we reclaim our bodies, honor our communities, and listen for our ancestors, we create futures where liberation isn't a concept—it's a rhythm.

Personal Reflection: The Light Within

Weeks before my stroke, during Advanced Somatic Experiencing training, my body had been whispering: fatigue that sleep couldn't touch, a band of tightness across my chest, headaches that overstayed their welcome. My body was speaking. I wasn't listening.

During a touch practice, I lay on the table as the "lender." The room was quiet: soft footsteps, a chair sliding gently across the floor, that particular training-room stillness where air feels attentive. A warm current rose through me, slow at first, then sure, like hands you trust lifting you from underneath. The warmth gathered at my sternum, then spread to my ribs, my throat, my face. My jaw unlatched. My breath widened.

Then came the light.

Eyes closed, I saw it, vivid, clean, radiant. Not a glow at the edges, but a wash of brightness pouring down and through me. Not imagined, not symbolic, but vivid, radiant light pouring through me as if someone had angled a lamp directly above my skin. It was so real I could feel it like warmth after winter. It was so present I could feel it on my skin, like sun after a long winter.

Without thinking, I spoke aloud:
"Where is that light coming from?"
No one answered. The room stayed steady, hands still gentle.
A few breaths later, stronger: "Do you see this? It's so bright. Where is the light?"
I asked again, three, maybe four times, because I needed confirmation.
The brightness felt undeniable, as real as the table beneath me.

When the practice ended, I opened my eyes expecting to see a lamp, a spotlight, a window shaft I'd somehow missed. My group looked puzzled, kind, a little concerned. One person said softly, "There wasn't any light over you." Another added, "No fixtures moved. Nothing changed in the room."

I scanned the ceiling, the walls, every corner. Nothing.

Heat rose behind my eyes—the kind that comes when you realize you've just touched something true. It wasn't out there. It was in here. The light wasn't shining on me—it was shining from me.

I sat up slowly, both embarrassed and awed, trying to reconcile the certainty of what my body knew with the blank, ordinary ceiling above me. Part of me wanted to dismiss it as imagination. Another part, the part that finally felt held, refused to explain it away. For once, I didn't abandon my own perception to match the room.

That moment became a touchstone in the weeks that followed, as my health unraveled and fear tried to take the wheel. When my chest clenched with uncertainty, I went back to the table in my mind: the warmth gathering, the breath widening, the light arriving like a promise. I would press my palm to my sternum and ask my body to remember. It did.

That light taught me something I didn't know I needed: my resilience doesn't live in performance or praise. It lives in my tissues, my breath, my belonging to myself. It showed me what somatic abolitionism has helped me claim, that I can release what was never mine to carry: the demand to be strong without rest, the silence that protects other people's comfort, the grief I inherited and tried to metabolize alone. And I can keep what is mine: ancestral steadiness at my back, a body that reaches for repair, a spirit that refuses to dim.

So when I say my body is not a burden and not a battleground, this is what I mean. My body is a sanctuary. A vessel of wisdom. A source of strength. A beacon of light, one I can feel even with my eyes closed.

Chapter 17
Somatic Abolitionism as Resistance for BIPOC Clinicians

Naming and Resisting the Weight

For us, the workplace is often where microaggressions, gatekeeping, and "be smaller" expectations collide. The toll is somatic—tight shoulders after meetings, shallow breath before supervision, migraines after being dismissed, nausea after "jokes" we're expected to ignore. The body keeps the score even when institutions refuse to keep records.

I know this weight. I carried it for years, convincing myself that more effort and less voice would keep me safe. Then I had a stroke. My body had been whispering for so long that it finally had to shout.

A Moment That Changed Me

In custody behavioral health, the days blurred together—heavy stories, metal doors, the hum of fluorescent lights that never dimmed. The work mattered to me. It still does. But one afternoon fractured something I had been holding together for far too long.

I stepped into the staff room—a space meant for decompression. Coffee cups half-drained, schedules taped to the wall, that faint buzz of exhaustion we all carried. At first, I wasn't really listening. My mind was somewhere between patients and paperwork. Then I caught it: laughter.

Not the weary laughter that comes from release, but something sharp, something cruel.

White clinicians were standing in a small circle, mocking Black inmates openly, mimicking speech patterns, twisting dialects, acting out exaggerated gestures, trading caricatures of pain for comedy. Their voices rose in rhythm, in sync, as if this performance were a kind of unspoken bonding ritual.

My body registered it before my mind did. My breath shortened; my hands went cold. A familiar current surged through my chest, the electric freeze that happens when your nervous system recognizes danger, even if your brain wants to rationalize it away. The air thickened. The laughter rang louder than it should have.

I froze.
My throat tightened.
Time bent.

My colleague, a Black clinician, stood beside me. I could feel his shoulders tense before his voice emerged, steady, calm, but pulsing with that ancient tremor of restrained fury:
"That's not okay."

The room went still.
Eyes darted.
Then someone chuckled nervously and said the words that branded themselves into my body:
"Oh—we're sorry. We didn't know you were in here."

Not sorry for the dehumanization.
Not sorry for the harm.
Sorry for being overheard.

Their apology wasn't repentance; it was self-preservation. And the silence that followed was heavier than the laughter that preceded it.

I remember the ache behind my sternum, that slow burn of humiliation and grief blending into disbelief. The kind of ache that makes you want to disappear and scream at the same time. My colleague met my eyes, no words, just knowing. A conversation older than either of us: *Here we are again.*

That night, I didn't sleep. The images replayed on a loop, my body restless with what it couldn't digest. I did what I had been trained to do, what I believed was right. I reported it.

The leader I turned to, a person of color, someone I trusted to understand, listened quietly, hands folded. His tone was almost tender when he said:
"Sometimes, we people of color have to make ourselves smaller in order to survive in these systems."

Smaller.
As if survival required self-erasure.
As if safety and silence were the same thing.

Those words landed in my body like a command I had followed all my life. And for the first time, I felt the full weight of it: how smallness had been mistaken for professionalism, how silence had been mistaken for strength.

Something inside me said, *No more.*

That day, I decided I would no longer shrink to fit into spaces that demanded my invisibility as a condition of belonging. I would no longer collude with my own diminishment to make others comfortable.

So, I resigned. Not as an act of rebellion, but as an act of reclamation. I left with my integrity intact, my spirit intact, my voice intact.

Walking away was not weakness. It was worship.
It was me choosing myself over a system that never chose me.
It was liberation in motion.

Somatic Reflection:
When the Body Knows Before Words Arrive

Pause here.

Think of a moment you felt dismissed, unseen, or erased.

Gently observe:

- Where does your body remember it?
- What happens to your breath?
- What sensations signal No?
- What sensations signal Yes, I'm here?

Place a hand over the place that holds the truth.

Whisper:
I do not have to make myself smaller to belong.

Feel your body register it, not as an idea, but as possibility.

Processing the Impact—In My Body

After that moment, my shoulders tensed for weeks; my chest stayed tight. Somatic abolitionism gave me a path back:

Feet grounded.
Breath steady.
Hand to heart with compassion.
Ancestors encircling me in memory.

The pain didn't evaporate, but clarity emerged:
I can resist harm without abandoning myself.

Rest as Defiance

Somatic abolitionism teaches that rest is not luxury—it is protest.
We are conditioned to be endlessly available, endlessly giving.
But our bodies are sacred, not instruments of extraction.

In a time of DEI rollbacks and institutional denial, tending to our bodies is resistance. Naming our truth is resistance. Refusing erasure is resistance.

Embodied commitments:

1. I listen when my body asks for pause.

2. I acknowledge pain instead of domesticating it.

3. I release what is not mine to carry.

4. I seek communities where my body is believed.

We are not here merely to endure.
We are here to live.

CHAPTER 18
INTEGRATING SOMATIC ABOLITIONISM INTO CLINICAL PRACTICE AND SELF-CARE

Somatic abolitionism is not just a theory; it is a way of practicing, a way of relating, a way of being in a body that has survived the unthinkable and still insists on rising. For BIPOC clients, racism and generational trauma are not distant concepts. They show up as tight jaws in meetings, shallow breaths in waiting rooms, burning behind the eyes when we're dismissed, and exhaustion that lingers for days.

Our work is to create rooms where bodies can finally exhale.
Where truth doesn't need translation.
Where safety isn't negotiated, it is felt.

Holding Space for Black & POC Clients

Create containers where clients can:

- Name racial harm without it being minimized or redirected.

- Notice where it lives in their body—the jaw, the chest, the gut, the breath.

- Regulate their system enough to choose their next step from steadiness, not survival.

Core tools, woven with care:

- Grounding

  Invite orientation to the present moment:
  feet on the ground, weight supported, eyes tracking something
  neutral or comforting.
  Grounding doesn't erase pain—it gives the body enough safety
  to meet it.

- Breathwork (choice-based)

  No counting, no forcing.
  Just slow, intentional exhales, gentle sighs, soft humming, breath
  as an invitation, not an instruction.

- Micro-movement

  Small shifts that signal safety:
  shoulder rolls, loosening the jaw, hand-to-heart, palm-to-sternum,
  subtle rocking.
  The body whispers: *I'm here. I'm safe enough to stay.*

- Titrated story work

  Touch the edge of the memory.
  Pause. Resource. Return.
  Trauma opens gently. Let the body lead the pace.

- Ancestral resourcing

  Invite the presence of those who made their life possible:
  a hand at the back, a song in the room, the warmth of someone
  who prayed them into existence.
  Belonging becomes sensation.

- Boundary practice

  Help the body rehearse its "no," its "not today," its exits
  and pauses—

stance, breath, eye line, voice.
Boundaries become muscle memory.

Self-Care for Clinicians

- Begin sessions with your body:
  Two minutes of orientation, three slow exhales, one sentence of intention.

- Close the loop after hard work:
  Shake, stretch, hum, step outside, let your system complete what it carried.

- Co-regulate with colleagues:
  Ten-minute debriefs that include breath and body, not just clinical notes.

- Protect your recovery time:
  Schedule rest the way you schedule court dates, deadlines, or intakes: nonnegotiable.

- Devotion to joy:
  One act every day that nourishes your spirit
  music, prayer, sunlight, laughter, a moment that feels like soft earth.

Practice Box: A 5-Minute Return-to-Body Ritual

1. Arrive:
   Feel your feet. Name five things you see.

2. Hand-to-Heart:
   Inhale gently; lengthen the exhale naturally. Repeat five times.

3. Micro-Move:
   Roll shoulders, unclench jaw, soften the belly.

4. Anchor Image:
   Call in an ancestor or elder who steadies you.

5. Choose:
   Ask: *What is one kind thing my body needs next?*
   Then honor it.

Four Roots Check-In

- Identity:
  Which parts of me feel tender today? Which feel strong?

- Story:
  What inherited narrative am I living right now?
  Is it still mine?

- Body:
  Where do I brace? Where do I soften?
  Where can I allow 1 percent more ease?

- System:
  What norms, policies, or dynamics are shaping my experience right now—and what boundary or support do I need in response?

Closing

Our bodies are not proof of endurance—they are proof that we are still here, still breathing, still becoming. When we root into ancestry, practice in community, and treat our bodies as sacred, healing becomes a daily, radical act.

Healing is not just possible—
it is ours.
I choose it.
Fully.
Unapologetically.
Sacredly.

CHAPTER 19
EMBODIED ABOLITION: HEALING, RESISTANCE, AND THE BODY

Why This Work Matters Now

We are living in a time that keeps asking us to shrink.
Diversity efforts rolled back. Affirmative action under attack.
Healing spaces stripped of color, language, and lineage.

For Black and Brown clinicians, this isn't theory; it's embodied reality.
We are asked to hold others' pain while systems quietly re-inflict our own.
We are told to keep showing up even as our bodies whisper, *no more.*

Somatic abolitionism becomes the map back to ourselves—
a compass that leads us toward what our bodies already know:
that healing and resistance are not opposites,
but two breaths in the same body.

It invites us to feel the pulse of Belonging,
to surrender into Yielding,
to rise again through Resilience,
and to break false peace through Disruption.

And through it all, our Four Roots—Identity, Story, Body, and System—
remind us where our healing grows.

Belonging—Reclaiming the Sacred in Culture

(Identity Root)

It wasn't a dramatic moment.
Just a phone call, a request for time—for care.
A close family member was being released from prison.
I needed the morning to pick him up.

In my world, that isn't optional. It's sacred.
It's how we welcome our own back into life.
The first face they see is ceremony—it's nervous system repair,
it's saying, *You are still ours.*

My supervisor didn't see it that way.
"Have someone else pick him up," she said.

I explained. I spoke from the rooted place:
how reentry is fragile, how family connection prevents collapse,
how culture *is* the container of healing.
She said, "If you call in, I'll write you up."

My breath shortened. Heat rose.
A pulse behind my eyes.
That ancient body knowledge flared—*danger.*
This was the same woman who once told me
that race, culture, and community don't matter in the healing process.

But my body knew otherwise.
It knew that belonging *is* medicine.
That family is regulation.
That to abandon culture is to abandon self.

That moment broke something open.
It was the collision of my Identity Root—Black, woman,

healer, daughter—
against a system that demanded neutrality where love belonged.

I chose my family. I went.
Not from rebellion, but reverence.
Because Belonging means returning to what the soul knows is sacred.

Yielding—Rest as Rebellion

(Body Root)

The fallout came as expected—emails, tension, paperwork.
My body began keeping score:
tight shoulders, shallow breath, restless sleep.
The cost of compliance was written in muscle and marrow.

Somatic abolitionism taught me to pause.
To Yield.

Yielding is not giving up; it is giving in to wisdom.
It's the quiet refusal to keep marching when your body begs for stillness.

I began again with the simplest tools:

- Grounding: feeling the floor beneath my feet.

- Breath: long exhale, soft sigh, letting sound loosen the grip.

- Touch: one hand over my sternum, one on my belly.

- Ancestral presence: closing my eyes until I could feel them—my people behind me, hands on shoulders, whispering, *rest, baby, rest.*

My Body Root began to thaw.
The tremor of fatigue turned to release.
The shaking was not weakness—it was the nervous system's way of returning to rhythm.

In that yielding, I heard the truth:
I do not have to earn rest.
I do not have to prove worthiness through exhaustion.
My rest is resistance. My pause is protest.

Resilience—The Body Remembers and Repairs

(Story Root)

When I returned to work, I hoped for understanding.
Instead, I was met with cold stares, tighter monitoring, and whispered
meetings I wasn't invited to.
Accusation replaced compassion. Silence replaced support.

I had sent my supervisor a letter of concern—hoping, still, that account-
ability might live somewhere in the system.
I believed that if I spoke my truth clearly and calmly, someone might
finally listen.
But instead of care, retaliation came.
My work was suddenly questioned. My intentions, distorted.
Emails dissected, tone policed, body watched.

Every interaction felt like walking through invisible tripwires—
one wrong step, one misinterpreted word, and I'd be framed as the problem instead of the person harmed.
The air thickened around me. The tension lived in my shoulders.
My body wanted to flee. My spirit wanted to fight.

What I experienced wasn't just professional scrutiny—it was a systemic
response to a Black woman's truth.
It was the old pattern playing out again:
speak up, get punished;
stand firm, get labeled;
demand dignity, get disciplined.

But my body refused to carry their distortion as my story.
A deeper voice—steady, ancient, and unmistakably mine—rose up
through the breath:
I am not small. I am sacred.

That was my Story Root reclaiming voice.
Resilience is not about enduring harm—it's about transforming it.
It is the body saying, *We survived. Now we will heal differently.*

Through breathwork, grounding, movement, and ritual,
I began to metabolize what the system tried to bury in me.
Each sigh became rebellion.
Each tremor, a truth untold.
Each prayer, each humming exhale, each night I chose rest over
rumination—
was my body's way of rewriting the story.

I stopped seeking validation from spaces that could not see me.
Instead, I listened to the wisdom pulsing inside my ribs—
the drumbeat of a lineage that refuses to vanish.

Disruption—Refusing Smallness

(System Root)

This time, I didn't resign.
My body did.

After months of pressure, retaliation, and disregard, my nervous system
finally reached its threshold.
It was as if my body, exhausted from holding the line alone, whispered the
truth I had been trying to rationalize:
Enough.

The stroke came on November 18, sudden, surreal, a breaking point
wrapped in stillness.

One moment I was working; the next, my body stopped negotiating.
My right side heavy, speech slurred, thoughts scattered like startled birds.
It wasn't betrayal. It was protest.

Because when the system refuses to hear our *no*, the body delivers
it for us.
When advocacy is punished and silence demanded, the body disrupts the
lie by collapsing the illusion of control.
This was not failure—it was physiology reclaiming truth.

In the language of the System Root, this was disruption in its
purest form:
not rebellion for rebellion's sake,
but the body enforcing boundaries that policy denied.

The system expected compliance.
My body gave consequence.

Lying in that hospital bed, I realized something I will never forget—
Disruption is not always loud.
Sometimes it's a shutdown, a sacred surrender, a full-body declaration
that survival can no longer mean self-abandonment.

Healing since then has been my revolution.
Every therapy session, every slow step, every breath reclaimed from fatigue
is resistance.
Each moment of rest is a manifesto: *I will not disappear to make you
comfortable.*

The System Root reminds us that the body and institution are
intertwined.
When systems harm us, our bodies carry the cost.
When our bodies break, they expose what the system refuses to see.

My stroke was not the end of me; it was my body's uprising.

A disruption born of wisdom.
A holy demand for rest, for justice, for repair.

Integrating Somatic Abolitionism in Practice

Somatic abolitionism isn't theory; it's a living clinical approach that restores humanity to therapy itself.

When we embody it, we:

- Name racialized harm without apology or minimization.

- Track physiology gently, helping clients notice where the wound lives.

- Honor culture as clinical, not optional.

- Model embodied truth: breathing, pausing, taking rest in real time.

It teaches clients to:

- Feel safety in their own rhythm.

- Release tension stored by generations of vigilance.

- Reconnect with ancestral wisdom.

- Reclaim voice and agency from systems that trained them to mute.

The Four Roots in Healing Practice

When clients begin to heal somatically, I guide them through these Four Roots:

1. Identity Root—Who am I within the system? Which parts of me were told not to belong here?

2. Story Root—What stories did I inherit, and which ones am I rewriting?

3. Body Root—Where does this story live in my body? What sensations tell the truth?

4. System Root—What external forces shaped these experiences, and how can I resist their residue through boundary, rest, and connection?

These questions become movement.
They help each client remember themselves—piece by piece, breath by breath.

BYRD in Motion: A Living Map for Liberation

Belonging—I chose family over policy.
Yielding—I let my body rest and release the lie of endless strength.
Resilience—I turned pain into embodied wisdom, rewriting the narrative of survival.
Disruption—I walked away from a system that demanded silence, choosing self-honor instead.

Each movement was guided by my Roots:
Identity grounded me,
Story evolved me,
Body repaired me,
System challenged me.

Together, they became both compass and commitment—
the practice of healing not just myself, but the soil my healing grows in.

Closing: The Body Refuses Erasure

I am not a burden.
I am not a battleground.
I am a sanctuary.

Every breath I take in truth disrupts an old system.
Every act of rest rewrites a rule.
Every moment of embodied belonging heals a lineage.

My resistance is rhythmic.
My healing is holy.
My work is alive.

And this body—this Black, breathing, sacred body—
will keep saying yes to life,
even when the world says I should be small.

CHAPTER 20
CREATING A CONTAINER FOR HEALING

Opening Reflection: Safety Reimagined

For many in the Black and POC communities, safety has never been a given—it has been something we *create*, not something the world simply offers. Safety, as defined by dominant systems, often feels distant or conditional: be quiet, be agreeable, be less of yourself.

But in somatic abolitionism—and in the BYRD Model—safety is not absence of threat.
It is *presence of connection*.
It is the sacred exhale that arrives when the body senses belonging again.

We are not chasing perfection; we are cultivating *possibility*.

It's not about eliminating every danger.
It's about creating spaces where the nervous system can loosen its grip.
It's about cultivating environments where the body can rest—even if only for a breath.

Creating a container for healing is an act of rebellion in a world that benefits from our exhaustion.
It means choosing to foster spaces—within ourselves, our sessions, our communities—where repair is possible, even when the world remains unwell.

Belonging—The Identity Root of Safety

When we create a container for healing, we begin with *Belonging*—the sacred reminder that we are not alone in our becoming.

Safety starts with being *seen*.
To belong is to feel our presence mirrored, not managed; our identity honored, not hidden.

For Black and BIPOC clinicians and clients, belonging asks us to reroot safety in culture and community:

- In the laughter that ripples through shared meals.
- In the cadence of our mother tongues.
- In the knowing glances that say, "I get it," without explanation.

Embodied Awareness Practice (Identity Root):
Pause.
Feel your body in the room.
Ask yourself:

- Where do I feel most at home within myself?
- What parts of me have been told to leave that home behind?
- Can I invite those parts back in?

Every time we reclaim our cultural rhythms, our language, our truths—we reenter belonging.
We create containers that reflect *who we are*, not who the system expects us to be.

Belonging is not a location. It's a frequency.
And when we attune to it, our clients do too.

Yielding—The Body Root of Safety

Healing cannot thrive in a body that is braced for harm.
To *Yield* is to soften, not to surrender, but to *allow*.

So many of us have learned to hold ourselves tight, to survive, to appear competent, to avoid harm.
But yielding is the body's way of saying, *I trust this moment enough to rest.*

Grounding Ritual (Body Root):

- Place one hand over your heart and one over your abdomen.
- Breathe slowly, letting your exhale extend longer than your inhale.
- Imagine the ground beneath you, solid, ancient, holding you.
- Whisper softly: *I am held.*

Yielding is sacred rest. It is the nervous system's reclamation of softness in a world that mistakes it for weakness.

When we yield, we create the conditions for the body to recalibrate—to move from defense to repair, from vigilance to vitality.

This is the work of the Body Root: teaching the body it no longer has to earn its right to relax.

Resilience—The Story Root of Safety

Creating a healing container also means allowing our stories to breathe.
Resilience is not pushing through pain, it is rewriting the story our bodies have been forced to tell.

Amid the George Floyd protests, while working in custody behavioral health, I felt this truth in my bones.
The world outside was burning with grief and rage. Inside, I sat across from men who carried the same trauma in their muscles, their breath,

their silence.
They carried both their own pain and the weight of history.
And I was trying to hold them while holding myself.

Safety, in that moment, was not about erasing danger.
It was about creating a *momentary refuge*, a pause long enough for breath to find us again.

Somatic Story Practice (Story Root):
Invite your body to tell the truth.

- Where does exhaustion live?
- Where does hope still hum?

Let movement emerge—a hand to your chest, a sigh, a slow sway.
That motion is your body's way of storytelling.

Resilience means letting the story evolve from survival to sovereignty.
It means saying: *My body remembers the harm, but it also remembers the healing.*

Every sigh, every tremor, every tear is a sacred punctuation mark in that rewriting.

Disruption—The System Root of Safety

To create a container for healing in systems that were never designed for our wholeness is an act of radical disruption.

We are not waiting for permission to rest anymore.
We are designing systems within systems—small circles of truth inside institutions built on silence.

Disruption here is gentle, not violent. It is a clinician taking a breath before responding to a microaggression.
It is refusing to spiritual-bypass racial pain.

It is naming oppression in supervision.

It is saying to a colleague, "Race matters here. Culture matters here. We matter here."

System Root Reflection:

- What power structures in my environment impact how I hold space?

- How can I resist replicating those structures in my practice?

- How can I model disruption through boundary, transparency, and truth?

Safety is not the absence of conflict—it is the presence of authenticity. When we disrupt with compassion, we make space for collective repair.

The Four Roots in Practice

The Four Roots ground the BYRD Model in lived, embodied practice:

1. Identity Root—Belonging: Reconnecting to cultural truth and communal safety.

2. Story Root—Resilience: Transforming survival narratives into embodied wisdom.

3. Body Root—Yielding: Restoring the nervous system through softness and awareness.

4. System Root—Disruption: Challenging structures that perpetuate harm through embodied integrity.

Together, these Roots anchor healing within the nervous system *and* the collective—reminding us that liberation is not individual work, but relational, rhythmic, and ancestral.

Closing Reflection: Creating Our Own Medicine

Safety will never be gifted to us by the systems that harmed us.
We must grow it from within, water it with community, and tend it
with rest.

So I ask you:

- Where does your body still brace for the world?
- What would it feel like to soften, even a little?
- What ancestral ritual reminds you that you are already whole?

Creating a container for healing is not a luxury—it's our lineage.
When we breathe together, hum together, remember together—
we become the medicine.

And when we do, the BYRD takes flight:

- Belonging returns us to each other.
- Yielding teaches us to trust the pause.
- Resilience writes new stories in the body.
- Disruption reshapes the world around us.

Our containers are not cages—they are sanctuaries.
Our bodies are not battlegrounds—they are altars.
And our healing, rooted in the sacred soil of ancestry and awareness,
is the most radical act of all.

CHAPTER 21
CREATING A CONTAINER FOR CLIENTS: HOLDING SPACE FOR HEALING

Opening Reflection

To hold space is to do holy work.
It is to say: *You can set your armor down here.*

For Black and BIPOC bodies, this act is nothing short of revolutionary.
Safety—the very thing therapy often promises—has rarely been promised
to us. It has had to be built, claimed, and remembered through the small,
steady practices of presence.

Safety, in this context, is not the absence of danger; it is the presence
of dignity.
It's the whisper our nervous systems long to hear: *You are not alone. You
are safe enough to exhale.*

Our bodies hold the memories of what the world has done to us—not
just personally, but generationally.
This is epigenetics in motion: the science of how inherited trauma shapes
biology, and how healing can reshape it again. The cortisol levels our
grandmothers carried, the inflammation our fathers endured, the hypervigilance passed down through generations—these are not metaphors.
They are patterns imprinted on the body's story.

But here is the miracle: *healing writes back.*
Each breath, each tremor, each act of rest becomes a new genetic possibility.
Our cells listen when we speak safety to them. Our breath rewrites what our blood once remembered.

To create a container for healing is to create the conditions for that rewriting—a space where the nervous system no longer rehearses danger, but rehearses belonging.

And so, we begin not as therapists holding clients, but as bodies remembering bodies.
We begin by rooting into the BYRD Model—because before we can build a container for others, we must embody one ourselves.

The BYRD Model as the Foundation for Healing Containers

Belonging.
Because no one heals in isolation. Belonging is the soil. It's the gentle hum beneath every therapeutic alliance: *You matter here.*
In practice, belonging looks like safety without performance—eye contact without demand, language without assumption, silence that welcomes instead of erases.

Yielding.
Because rest is resistance. To yield is to remember that slowing down is sacred.
We do not rush our clients' healing. We move at the speed of trust, at the rhythm of the body.
Yielding means allowing pauses, honoring pacing, and trusting the body's innate wisdom.

Resilience.

Because our strength is not new; it's inherited.

Resilience in the room is not about "pushing through"—it's about *returning home.*

It's the nervous system remembering that safety is possible again, one regulated breath at a time.

Disruption.

Because systems need shaking, not just softening.

Creating healing containers means naming injustice out loud—refusing to spiritualize or pathologize pain that was never personal to begin with.

It means disrupting silence with truth, so the body no longer has to carry what the world refuses to see.

Each pillar of the BYRD Model holds the four Roots of Healing beneath it:

Story, Body, System, and Identity

When we hold space, these roots intertwine like tendrils beneath the surface—unseen, but essential.

- Story Root: invites clients to speak the unspeakable, to reclaim narrative authority.

- Body Root: honors the nervous system as sacred text.

- System Root: confronts how power, policy, and prejudice shape the very air our clients breathe.

- Identity Root: connects us back to meaning, ritual, and the sacredness of existence.

When all four roots are engaged, the container becomes more than a clinical room—it becomes a sanctuary.

A space where the body can finally whisper: *I am safe enough to remember. I am safe enough to release.*

Holding Space in an Unsafe World

For Black and BIPOC clinicians, holding space often means creating refuge within institutions that were never built for us.
We are the bridge between collective pain and individual transformation, tasked with holding what the system ignores while carrying the echoes of our own lineage.

Holding space is not about fixing.
It's about *feeling with*, being fully present to what unfolds without rushing it toward resolution.

It means sitting in the fire with our clients and trusting that the body knows how to find its way back to water.

This kind of holding requires more than skill—it requires soul stamina. And it begins, always, with presence.

1. Presence and Attunement: The Art of Being Fully Here

Presence is not performance. It is permission.
Permission for the client to bring their full self into the room because we have brought ours.

Before every session, ground yourself:

- Place one hand on your sternum, one on your stomach.

- Breathe in through your nose, out through your mouth.

- Feel your feet.

- Ask your body, *Am I here?*

Our nervous systems are instruments of attunement. Clients, especially those with trauma histories, can sense dysregulation in us even before words are spoken.

When we are fragmented, they feel it. When we are steady, they breathe deeper.

Presence is a somatic act.
It tells the client's body: *You are not alone in this.*

Clinical Reflection:

"How does my own nervous system show up when my client is in distress?
Where do I brace, tighten, or flee internally, and how can I return to regulation without abandoning the moment?"

In the language of the BYRD Model:

- Presence is Belonging made visible.

- Attunement is Yielding to the rhythm of another nervous system.

- Co-regulation is Resilience embodied.

- Staying grounded amid discomfort is Disruption in action.

2. Dismantling the Hierarchy of Healing—Naming Power, Restoring Agency

The therapy room is not neutral.
For Black and Brown clients, it often echoes with the ghosts of medical racism, coercion, and erasure.
If we do not name power, it quietly shapes every exchange.

To hold space ethically, we must dismantle hierarchy—not by pretending it doesn't exist, but by naming it with humility.

Say aloud:

"This space belongs to you, too.
If something I say doesn't feel right, you can tell me.
You get to decide the pace of your healing."

Agency is the nervous system's language of freedom.
When clients sense that they have choice, in movement, in silence, in story, their bodies begin to soften. The fight, flight, and freeze mechanisms loosen. Safety begins to write itself into the body's code.

This, too, is epigenetic repair.
Because agency reactivates neural pathways silenced by domination.

3. Grounding Practices—Preparing the Body for Depth and Return

Trauma is a full-body story.
Grounding is how we translate that story back into safety.

Before deep work:
Invite stillness. Breathe together.

"Can you feel your feet on the floor?
Can you sense where your body meets support?"

During moments of overwhelm:

"Would it feel okay to look around the room? Notice what feels stable, what feels steady."
"Would it help to place your hand over your heart, to remind your body you are here, now?"

After intense sessions:
Offer somatic closure.

"Let's take a moment to stretch. Feel your spine lengthen. Let your exhale be a release."

These grounding rituals are more than techniques—they are embodied theology.

They teach the nervous system that regulation is possible, that safety can be *practiced.*

In BYRD language:

- Grounding returns us to Body Root, where awareness becomes medicine.

- It honors Yielding, the sacred pause that precedes transformation.

- It builds Resilience, a cellular memory of safety.

- And it supports **Disruption**—interrupting inherited survival patterns and systems of harm by teaching the body that collapse is no longer required for change.

Each exhale whispers to our DNA: *You can rest now. The danger has passed.*

4. Inviting Cultural and Ancestral Strengths, Reclaiming the Wisdom Within

Many BIPOC clients don't need to *learn* healing—they need to *remember* it.

The rituals are already in their blood: humming, prayer, rhythm, story-telling, gathering, laughter that shakes the room.

Ask:

"What helps your body remember peace?"
"Who in your lineage carried strength that you draw from?"
"Would it feel meaningful to bring any of that wisdom into our work together?"

When clients reconnect with ancestral practices—drumming, movement, cooking, dance, ritual—they're not just engaging in nostalgia; they're participating in epigenetic restoration.

Every time we return to ancestral rhythm, we remind our nervous systems that the story didn't begin with trauma; it began with wholeness.

Clinical Note:
Honoring ancestral wisdom honors Spirit Root.
It invites the sacred into the session, where the clinical becomes
ceremonial.

5. Cocreating Boundaries—The Edges That Hold Safety

Boundaries are not walls; they are the edges that keep the container intact.
For trauma survivors, boundaries are often blurred, violated by others or
abandoned in the name of survival.

In therapy, boundaries model self-trust.
They teach clients that safety does not mean control; it means clarity.

Ask:

"What helps you feel safe here?"
"Would you like to take a break if things feel too intense?"
"What do you need to know about how we'll handle sensitive topics?"

Boundaries are acts of liberation, small, sacred no's that teach the body
how to say yes to safety.

When the Healer Is the Mirror— The Body-to-Body Dialogue

As clinicians, we are mirrors, reflecting the possibility of safety through
our own embodiment.
But mirrors get fogged when unacknowledged pain remains inside us.

Every client who trembles reminds us of our own unprocessed fear.
Every silence calls up our old survival strategies.
This is countertransference not as flaw, but as invitation, to tend to what
arises in us without shame.

The BYRD Model offers a map for this inner tending:

- Belonging: When you feel disconnected from your client, ask, "Where have I abandoned myself?"

- Yielding: When you feel urgency to fix, pause. The body heals at the speed of trust.

- Resilience: When compassion fatigue sets in, return to your breath. The ancestors breathed you here.

- Disruption: When systemic harm repeats itself in supervision or policy, name it out loud. Refusal is a form of care.

This inner reflection prevents reenactment and keeps your container clean, a space where both clinician and client can breathe.

Epigenetics and the Inheritance of Safety

Let's return to the science as story because the body has always been telling it.

Epigenetics teaches us that trauma does not vanish when the event ends; it lingers as instruction.
When a body experiences prolonged stress or terror, the nervous system sends chemical messengers—stress hormones like cortisol and adrenaline—to prepare for survival. Over time, those signals leave traces. They do not alter our DNA sequence, but they influence which genes are activated or silenced.

This process is called methylation, tiny molecular tags attaching themselves to our genetic code, marking the sites where stress once lived. These markers shape how our bodies respond to the world:
how easily we startle, how long it takes to calm, how deeply we sleep, how much inflammation we carry.

Science calls this epigenetic inheritance—the way stress responses are passed down through generations. But long before laboratories named it, our grandmothers already knew. They didn't call it methylation; they called it *spirit inheritance.*

They understood that the body keeps score in ways the mind cannot.
That a trembling hand at the dinner table might belong not only to the present, but to a lineage that learned trembling as prayer, as vigilance, as survival.
That a racing heart might carry the echo of flight, of ancestors who had to run, hide, or endure.

Epigenetics simply gives language to what our elders have whispered all along:
what happens to one generation lives, unspoken, in the next until someone turns toward it with love.

And love, too, is biochemical.
When we soothe, sing, or exhale together, we are not just calming emotion; we are recalibrating the body's molecular memory.
Every steady breath lowers cortisol, every safe connection softens the amygdala's alarm, every belly laugh releases oxytocin—signaling to our genes that the danger has passed.

This is the science of belonging.
Safety, practiced over time, can rewrite the epigenetic script.
It doesn't erase history, but it tells the body, *You no longer have to live inside its fear.*

When a Black mother rocks her child while humming the same hymn her grandmother hummed through segregation, she is doing epigenetic repair.
When a clinician of color slows their breathing before a session, grounding themselves in ancestral rhythm, they are doing epigenetic repair.
When a survivor allows their body to tremble and release instead of holding tension in silence, they are doing epigenetic repair.

Healing becomes a quiet rebellion against what was once encoded
in survival.
We are teaching our bodies new possibilities: safety without vigilance,
strength without armor, rest without guilt.

Our nervous systems whisper to our genes:

"You are safe now. You can stand down."

That whisper becomes the new inheritance.
Because safety, like trauma, is contagious; it ripples through relationships,
families, and communities.

Each moment of regulation is a love letter written in biology.
Each grounded breath is a message to the future, spoken in the language of peace.

And one day, generations from now, a descendant may find herself
breathing easier without knowing why
not realizing that somewhere in her lineage, someone—perhaps you
took a long, steady breath
and changed everything.

Clinician Care—Tending to the Healer Within

We cannot invite others into safety if we have forgotten what it feels like
in our own bodies.
As healers, we often carry the residue of other people's pain stories that
seep beneath the skin, tremors that echo in our sleep, sorrow that sits
behind our smiles.
We bear witness not just to trauma, but to its *frequency*—the low, steady
hum of suffering that can reverberate through our nervous systems if we
do not tend to it.

This is not failure.
It is physiology.

Our bodies, wired for connection, mirror the pain we hold space for.
When our clients tremble, we may feel the echo in our own muscles.
When they cry, something in our chest tightens in recognition.
This is co-regulation—the nervous systems of two beings syncing
in empathy.
It's a gift, but without grounding, it becomes an inheritance of
exhaustion.

Healing requires boundaries, not because we are detached, but because
we are sacred.
We cannot pour endlessly from a well we never refill.

Belonging: Remembering You Are Not Alone

In the BYRD Model, *Belonging* begins with remembering that the healer
is also human.
We belong not only to our profession but to a lineage—a web of healers, elders, and ancestors who stood in the same fire and refused to
be consumed.

Belonging reminds us that the act of holding space is communal, even
when we are alone in our office or behind a telehealth screen.
Every time we exhale, we breathe with those who came before us: the
midwives, the medicine women, the freedom fighters, the spiritual guides,
those who prayed for a day we could sit in rooms like these, helping others find their way home.

Let this remembrance soften you.
Let it be the hand on your back when you begin to doubt your capacity.

Reflection:

"Who holds me when I am holding others?"

"Where does my lineage of healing begin, and how can I call upon it when I feel alone?"

Community is not optional; it is medicine.
Isolation breeds burnout. Connection cultivates resilience.

Yielding: Rest as Resistance

In a world that glorifies productivity, *Yielding* is radical.
To yield is to rest without guilt, to pause without apology.
It is to remember that slowing down is not failure; it's repair.

Rest recalibrates the vagus nerve, rebalances cortisol, and repairs immune function.
Each moment of genuine rest, sleep, stillness, or sacred idleness tells the body, *You are safe enough to stop bracing.*

The truth is, many Black and BIPOC clinicians carry ancestral patterns of overwork.
Our nervous systems have been trained to stay vigilant, to "earn" rest through exhaustion.
But exhaustion is not a badge of honor; it's a wound disguised as worth.

So we reclaim rest as a practice of healing, a small rebellion against a world that has always demanded our labor but rarely offered our liberation.

Practice:

- Before each session, close your eyes.

- Take three deep breaths, longer on the exhale.

- Whisper to your body: *You are allowed to rest, even while you work.*

Resilience: Rebuilding from the Inside Out

Resilience is not a call to endure. It is a call to evolve.
It is not about "bouncing back" but about returning differently, wiser, slower, softer.

The nervous system learns through repetition. Every moment of grounding, every deep exhale, every mindful pause teaches the body a new pattern.
This is neuroplasticity as sacred ritual.

When we practice resilience intentionally, we strengthen our capacity to hold space without losing ourselves.
We begin to trust that we can meet intensity with steadiness, that we can feel deeply and still remain rooted.

Somatic Practice for Resilience:

- Stand with your feet shoulder-width apart.

- Feel the ground beneath you, solid and unwavering.

- Inhale deeply through your nose, feeling your ribs expand.

- Exhale slowly through your mouth, imagining roots extending downward.

- With each exhale, release what is not yours to carry.

This is resilience in action; the body learning to stand tall without hardening.

Disruption: Saying No as a Sacred Act

Every healer working within oppressive systems faces a reckoning, the choice to either adapt to harm or disrupt it.
Disruption, in the BYRD Model, is not chaos; it is clarity.
It is the refusal to participate in your own depletion.

There will be times when you are asked to absorb too much: too many clients, too little pay, too little acknowledgment.
There will be moments when your silence will be expected, when you will be told, implicitly or directly, to "stay in your place."

Disruption is the body's quiet rebellion.
It is the "no" that protects your nervous system.
It is the boundary that says, *My body will not be a battlefield for broken systems.*

Reflection:

"Where in my work have I been asked to shrink?"
"What would it look like to choose my well-being over compliance?"

Each act of refusal is a form of epigenetic healing, the undoing of a survival script written by oppression.
When we say no, we are teaching our cells that safety no longer requires silence.

When the Healer's Body Speaks

There comes a moment, sometimes quiet, sometimes catastrophic, when the healer's body says, *Enough.*
It may come as exhaustion, illness, forgetfulness, tears that surprise you in the middle of a session.
It may come as shaking hands, a chest that won't unclench, a mind suddenly fogged from carrying too much for too long.

But even in that rupture, there is invitation.

The body does not betray us
it protects us
when we refuse to protect ourselves.

It demands slowness.

It demands care.
It demands truth.

It speaks through fatigue, through stillness, through the inability to push one more step down a path that no longer fits.
It calls us inward, back to breathe, back to presence, back to the parts of ourselves we abandoned in the name of being strong.

The body's "no" is not a failure
it is a boundary.
A wisdom.
A sacred insistence that healing must begin at home.

Recovery, in whatever form it takes, becomes a teacher.
One that speaks through the quiet, through the small movements, through the soft permission to rest.
It is the body's way of insisting on belonging again.

Reclaiming the Healer's Epigenetic Inheritance

When we care for ourselves, we do more than prevent burnout—we interrupt centuries of exploitation that taught us to equate worth with sacrifice.
This is epigenetic reclamation: transforming the molecular memory of survival into one of safety, joy, and ease.

Every nap taken, every boundary held, every belly laugh shared with loved ones is a message to our descendants:

"You will not inherit my exhaustion."
"You will not inherit my silence."
"You will inherit my peace."

Our ancestors endured so we could exhale.
We rest so our descendants can rise.

Closing Reflection: The Healer's Breath

Place your hand on your heart.
Take one deep, slow breath.
Feel the rise and fall—the steady rhythm of life choosing itself again
and again.

Whisper softly:

My healing is holy.
My rest is revolutionary.
My breath is the bridge between my ancestors and my descendants.

Because it is.

Every time you regulate your nervous system, you are tending to the nervous system of the collective.
Every time you choose gentleness, you are undoing generations of
inherited fear.
Every time you honor your body's limits, you are teaching the world what
liberation feels like.

And that is how the healer heals the lineage.
Not through endless giving, but through embodied remembering.

Chapter 22
The Challenge of Holding Space in Injustice

Opening Reflection:
The Weight of the World on Black Shoulders

Holding space in a world built on inequity is not just an act of care—it is an act of *defiance*.

It is the sacred, weary art of breathing in spaces that were not designed for our breath.

It is the refusal to disappear, even when every signal in the room tells us to make ourselves small.

And for Black clinicians, for Black healers, for Black bodies, the cost is steep.

The very systems that harm us still demand that we show up in service, polished and composed.

They ask us to absorb, to soothe, to fix, all while we are quietly bleeding inside.

They praise our resilience while feeding on it.

They applaud our professionalism while policing our tone.

They welcome our healing, but not our truth.

And yet, somehow, we still find a way to hold space.

To create sanctuaries of tenderness within institutions built on harm.

To turn our exhaustion into empathy, our grief into guidance.

That, too, is resistance.

A Childhood Lesson in Safety and Cruelty

I have known what it feels like to believe you are safe, only to be reminded that you are not.

I was a little girl when I first learned what it meant to be unsafe while doing nothing wrong.
My family was driving to my aunt's cabin in Lake Tahoe, the snow thick and glittering, the air sharp and quiet. My father's hands gripped the steering wheel steady, a man used to navigating not only icy roads but a world that didn't always make room for him.

Then the tires slipped.
The car slid over a small edge and came to rest off the side of the road. We weren't hurt, but we were stuck, surrounded by snow, stranded in the stillness of white silence. My father carried one of my sisters, my mother carried the other, and I walked beside them as we climbed back up toward the highway, our breaths forming small clouds in the frozen air.

We started walking, hoping someone would stop. The snow fell harder. The wind bit at our faces. Then, after what felt like forever, a snowplow appeared, orange lights flashing, rumbling down the road. Relief bloomed in my chest. Help was here.

The driver slowed, stopped his truck just ahead of us. My father stepped forward, waving. For a moment, I saw something soften in his shoulders— that fragile exhale that comes when you think you might finally be safe.

Then the man rolled down his window.
He looked right at us, a Black family, stranded and shivering on the side of the road, and smirked.

"Y'all better be careful out here," he said. Then, with a tone that cut colder than the snow itself, he added, "You niggers could get yourselves killed."

Before we could react, he slammed the truck into gear and turned the plow toward us. A wave of snow surged forward, crashing over our boots and coats, coating our faces with ice. My body jolted at the shock; my mother's arm came around me instinctively, pulling me close.

The man laughed, that sound I'll never forget, and drove away, the orange lights fading into the white distance.

We stood there, wet and frozen, the silence after his laughter louder than the storm. My father's jaw tightened, his breath coming heavy through the cold. My mother brushed the snow from my face, her voice low and trembling as she said, "Keep walking."

And we did. Step by step, down that endless road, soaked and stunned but moving forward because we had to.

After a while, headlights appeared again, another car slowing beside us. A white couple stepped out, their faces open with concern.
"Are you all right?" the woman asked, already wrapping a blanket around my shoulders. They didn't ask for an explanation. They didn't question our presence. They just helped, brushing snow off our coats, offering warmth, offering humanity.

That night, at the couple's cabin, my clothes finally dry, I lay awake replaying it all.
The laughter.
The snow.
The cruelty.
The kindness.

My body trembled beneath the blankets long after the cold had gone. Even as a child, I understood something words could never quite hold: The world could be cruel, but kindness existed, too.

That was my first lesson in holding space, not as a therapist, but as a witness.
To harm and to help.

To the weight of hate and the power of presence.
And even then, my body knew: sometimes the smallest acts of humanity keep us alive long enough to find our way home.

Holding Space as an Act of Resistance

As a Black woman, a clinician, a healer, I learned early that holding space is not neutral work.
It is political. It is embodied. It is ancestral.

To hold space in unjust systems is to carry an impossible contradiction:
How do I offer sanctuary to others while surviving the storm myself?
How do I hold space for my clients' grief when I am still healing from my own?
How do I stay grounded when the very ground beneath me is cracking?

For me, the answer lies in returning to what I learned that night in the snow.
I do not have to rescue everyone.
I do not have to fix every injustice.
I do not have to carry what my body cannot hold.

But I *can* bear witness.
I *can* stand beside someone in their pain.
I *can* create a moment of stillness in the middle of the storm, where someone else's breath, even for a second, can find safety.

And in that sacred reciprocity, I remind myself that I, too, deserve to be held.

The BYRD Model in Motion

When I hold space inside systems that demand silence, I root myself in the BYRD Model because it was born from this tension, this lived reality of being both healer and target.

- Belonging reminds me that I am not an outsider in my own body. Even when systems deny me belonging, I claim it through community, through ancestral lineage, through the knowing that I am part of something unbreakable.

- Yielding teaches me that slowing down is not defeat; it's survival. I can rest without guilt. I can pause without shame. I can choose softness in a world that worships hardness.

- Resilience is not about being unbreakable; it's about rebuilding differently.
  It is the alchemy of turning generational pain into embodied wisdom.

- Disruption is the whisper that becomes a roar: *I will not shrink to make you comfortable.*
  I will speak truth even when my voice shakes. I will model liberation in the way I take up space.

Together, these pillars create a living framework, a container that allows me to keep showing up without losing myself.

Chapter 23
Techniques to Create Safer and More Grounded Space

When safety cannot be promised, we build *safer* spaces, places where the nervous system can rest, where the spirit can remember home. Each practice here is rooted in culture, ancestry, and the somatic wisdom of Black and Brown bodies that have always known how to survive and repair.

Grounding Techniques for Stability

Grounding is how we come back to ourselves.
It's the body's declaration: *I am here. I have not been erased.*

1. Environmental Orientation with Cultural Anchors

Look around your space, not just to orient, but to affirm identity. Bring in ancestral art, family photos, kente cloth, or a bowl of Florida water. **Florida Water** is a scented cologne that has long been used in many Black, Caribbean, and Latinx healing traditions as a tool for clearing, grounding, and transition. It is often used to mark a moment of release, protection, or renewal—before prayer, after grief, or when the body needs help letting go. From a somatic perspective, scent can calm and orient the nervous system, offering safety and regulation without words. Florida Water is not about superstition; it is about ritual, intention, and honoring the body's need for sensory cues to feel settled and supported. These objects are more than décor, they are *reminders of continuity* in a system that thrives on fragmentation.

2. Breath Awareness with Affirmation

Pair each breath with an ancestral invocation:

Inhale—"I am held by those who came before me."
Hold—"Their strength flows through me."
Exhale—"I release what is not mine to carry."

This is more than mindfulness; it's reclamation. The breath becomes a bridge between generations, a quiet defiance of erasure.

3. Somatic Anchors with Symbolism

Place your hand over your heart, feeling the pulse that outlived oppression.
Feel your own warmth and imagine your ancestors' hands layered on top of yours, steady, patient, eternal.

4. Connection with the Earth through Ritual

Stand barefoot on the ground, dirt, grass, or floor, and imagine roots extending from your soles deep into the soil.
Say aloud:

"I stand on the shoulders of those who endured.
Their wisdom is my foundation. Their love is my shelter."

This is grounding as prayer. Grounding as protest. Grounding as *return*.

Creating Boundaries in Professional Spaces

Boundaries are not walls; they are *containers for dignity.*
For Black clinicians navigating microaggressions and systemic inequities, boundaries are sacred technology, the architecture that protects our nervous systems from collapse.

1. Protecting Your Energy with Symbolic Rituals

Before entering meetings or difficult environments, hold a small token of significance—a stone, a piece of fabric, a charm—and whisper,

"I am surrounded by divine protection. No harm can penetrate my peace."

These small rituals ground the body before the system can unground it.

2. Intentional Pauses with Ancestral Practices

Between sessions, burn sage or light a candle, if you can.
If you cannot, close your eyes for sixty seconds and imagine a warm glow enveloping you.
Breathe in renewal; exhale the residue of other people's pain.

3. Community-Driven Support Systems

Build circles of solidarity, colleagues, friends, or faith communities who speak your language of survival.
If such a space doesn't exist, create one. Healing doesn't happen in isolation; it happens in chorus.

Personal Reflection: The Stone I Still Carry

During one particularly heavy week at work, I found myself unraveling quietly, too many sessions, too little rest, too much injustice to metabolize.
My supervisors dismissed my concerns.
Colleagues questioned my judgment with a politeness that stung more

than open hostility.
I was praised for my "calm under pressure," but inside, I was shaking.

In those moments, I began carrying a small, smooth stone in my pocket,
the same one I had picked up all those years ago after that snowstorm in
Lake Tahoe.
Its surface was cool and polished, shaped by time and water,
much like me.

When meetings turned hostile or I felt invisible, I would reach for it.
I would rub my thumb across its surface and remember:
the cold, the cruelty, the survival.
The laughter that cut through the air.
The kindness that followed.
The way my father brushed off snow, and dignity, and still got us home.

That stone became my ritual of resilience.
It carried the memory of harm, but also the evidence of help.
It reminded me that even in the face of hatred, there is always humanity
somewhere, and that I, too, could be that for others.

Each time I touched it, I remembered who I came from
people who refused to disappear.
People who loved, even in frost.
People who knew that strength doesn't always roar; sometimes it whispers through a steady breath and a pocket-sized stone.

Closing Reflection: The Sacred Act of Care

Creating safer spaces within systems of injustice is not a luxury; it is
sacred labor.
It's the everyday miracle of choosing to stay tender in a world that keeps
asking us to harden.
It's the practice of turning ancestral pain into embodied prayer.

It's the belief that even when the world is unkind, we can still choose to be kind, to ourselves and to each other.

When I hold space now, I think of my father's hands brushing snow.
I think of the couple who stopped.
I think of that stone, still smooth, still solid.
And I remind myself:

We are the proof that healing and harm can coexist, but healing can win.
We are the living resistance, the embodied lineage of those who refused to die in despair.
And every time we hold space, we whisper back to the storm:

"You will not bury us. We know how to dig ourselves out."

CHAPTER 24
BUILDING A PERSONAL
PRACTICE SPACE

The BYRD Model in Motion:
Creating Sanctuary in a System That Drains

The Importance of a Safer Space for Healing

For Black bodies, and for all bodies marked by generational harm, creating a personal practice space is not indulgence; it's *reclamation.*
It's a way of saying, *My body deserves softness. My spirit deserves to breathe.*

For BIPOC clinicians, this space is more than décor or design; it's a lifeline, a quiet refusal against a world that keeps us in survival mode. Our healing space becomes the altar where we remember what the system tried to make us forget: we are sacred, we belong, and our rest is resistance.

When I enter my own healing space, I am met by symbols that whisper to my lineage. Elephants stand around me, ancient, grounded, remembering. They are my teachers in *Yielding*: knowing when to rest, when to roar, and when to simply stand still.
Each one holds a story. Their presence reminds me that strength is not a posture; it's a rhythm passed through blood and bone.

I light a candle, trace my fingers along the grooves of its holder, and breathe into my belly. My space smells faintly of sage and cocoa butter. Photos of my daughters line the table, faces full of future. This is not decoration; this is devotion.
Every item, every scent, every whisper in this space tells my nervous system: *You are home. You are safe. You do not need to shrink here.*

Creating Your Personal Healing Space through the BYRD Roots

Each aspect of the BYRD Model offers a root for how we build spaces that restore us.

1. Belonging—Rooting in Ancestral Connection

Belonging begins with remembering that we were never meant to heal in isolation. Our ancestors created circles of song and ritual long before the term "self-care" existed.

When you create your healing space, call them in.

- Display something that connects you to your people—beads, fabric, a photo, a line of poetry.

- Speak their names aloud when you enter.

- Let your body feel their presence behind you, reminding you that you do not walk this path alone.

Belonging whispers: *You are the continuation of a long line of healers.*

2. Yielding—Resting as Resistance

Yielding means giving your nervous system permission to surrender its vigilance.

In a society that glorifies exhaustion, rest is a radical act.

- Lie down when your body says "enough."

- Breathe slowly until your shoulders drop and your jaw unclenches.

- Keep a soft blanket nearby that feels like being held by someone who loves you.

Yielding says: *You do not have to earn your rest.*

3. Resilience—Building Strength through Ritual

Resilience isn't about pushing harder—it's about returning home to the body again and again.

Create rituals that remind you that you are not broken, even when the world feels unkind.

- Light a candle each morning and dedicate its flame to something you're reclaiming.

- Keep a journal where your tears and triumphs share the same page.

- Move—stretch, sway, or dance—to remind your body it still belongs to you.

Resilience affirms: *What was meant to break you has only made you deeper.*

4. Disruption—Protecting the Sacred

Disruption means setting boundaries that guard your peace.

When we protect our space, we disrupt the lie that Black women must always be available, accommodating, or strong.

- Say no without apology.

- Turn off your phone when you need silence.

- Refuse to let systems that exploit you dictate how you heal.

Disruption declares: *I am not here to be consumed. I am here to be whole.*

Adapting to Unpredictable Environments

Many of us don't have consistent access to stillness. The world follows us, emails pinging, demands knocking. But we can carry small sanctuaries with us, *pockets of peace stitched into the fabric of our days.*

- Grounding Object: A smooth stone, a shell from your grandmother's beach, or a bracelet that hums with memory.

- Portable Ritual: Two deep breaths at a stoplight. A whispered prayer before entering a meeting.

- Imaginal Space: Close your eyes and picture your grandmother's kitchen, or the porch where laughter once echoed. Feel that belonging in your body.

Even when space cannot be built, it can be *remembered*.

Epigenetic Healing: Writing Safety into Our Cells

Science calls it *epigenetics*, how experience and environment shape which genes wake or sleep. But for Black bodies, this is more than science; it's *ancestral conversation*.

Our ancestors endured unspeakable harm, yet somehow encoded strength in the same breath. Their survival became our inheritance, their regulation written into our DNA.

When we rest, when we breathe deeply, when we hum or rock or pray—
we are sending new messages through the bloodstream.
We are teaching our cells a different song:

"You are safe now. You can exhale."

Each act of self-care is a rewrite of history at the molecular level—a love letter to the future written in the language of the nervous system.

BYRD Somatic Practices for Daily Restoration

Reclaiming the Body as Home

Our bodies are both map and compass, carrying not only the memories of what we've endured but also the wisdom of how to return home.
These practices are invitations to pause, to listen, and to reconnect to your roots, Belonging, Yielding, Resilience, and Disruption.
Each practice can be done anywhere: in your healing corner, between sessions, or even in the quiet inhale before you speak truth to power.

1. Belonging—Remembering You Are Not Alone

Root: Identity + Story

This practice honors connection, to ancestors, community, and the self who still believes in wholeness.

Practice: "The Line Behind Me"

1. Sit or stand.

2. Close your eyes and imagine the people who came before you standing behind you—parents, grandparents, ancestors whose names you may never know but whose breath is in your lungs.

3. Feel their hands on your shoulders, steady and warm.

4. Whisper:

   I am my ancestors' dream realized. I belong to a story of survival and sacredness.

5. Let that belonging settle into your body, into the muscles that have carried too much alone.

When to Use:
Before stepping into white-dominant or high-stress spaces. When you start to doubt that your presence matters. When the room makes you feel like an exception instead of an inheritance.

2. Yielding—The Sacred Act of Softening

Root: Body

Yielding is the gentle surrender of the body's armor. It is not giving up, it's giving *in* to safety.

Practice: "The Weighted Breath"

1. Place one hand over your heart and one over your belly.

2. Inhale slowly through your nose for four counts. Exhale through your mouth for six.

3. As you exhale, imagine laying down one invisible stone you've been carrying—the expectation to be perfect, to be strong, to be unbreakable.

4. Whisper:

Rest is not a reward. It's my birthright.

5. Feel your body yield into gravity, shoulders lowering, breath deepening.

When to Use:
After difficult sessions. When your body feels tense from code-switching or chronic vigilance. When the world demands speed but your soul needs slowness.

3. Resilience—Returning to Yourself Again and Again

Root: Story + Body

Resilience is not about bouncing back, it's about expanding your capacity to stay connected while you heal.

Practice: "The Sound of My Own Strength"

1. Find a quiet place. Sit with your spine upright but relaxed.

2. Hum a single note, low and steady, feeling the vibration in your chest.

3. Let that vibration spread through your ribs, your throat, your skull.

4. Repeat:

"I am still here. My breath is proof."

5. When you finish, take a deep inhale and exhale with a sigh, releasing what's ready to leave.

When to Use:
After witnessing trauma in clients. When grief feels louder than hope. When you need to remember that your body has already survived everything it's lived through.

4. Disruption—Protecting the Sacred Within

Root: System

Disruption is the act of drawing a sacred boundary, refusing to collude with your own depletion.

Practice: "The Boundary Blessing"

1. Stand tall with your feet grounded.

2. Slowly sweep your hands from your head to your toes, as if brushing off dust or energy that isn't yours.

3. Say aloud:

    "What is mine, I keep. What is not mine, I release."

4. Picture a soft golden light encircling you—not a wall, but a gentle membrane of protection.

5. Breathe into that light until you feel its warmth settle at your center.

When to Use:
Before entering spaces where you anticipate microaggressions or racial fatigue. After difficult conversations where you feel unseen. When you need to return to your own sacred rhythm.

Daily Integration: A BYRD Reflection Practice

At the end of each day, spend five minutes journaling or reflecting on these prompts:

- Belonging: Where did I feel most connected to myself or others today?

- Yielding: Where did I allow my body to rest or soften?

- Resilience: What moment reminded me of my own strength?

- Disruption: What boundary did I honor today, or what boundary needs my attention tomorrow?

Let this be your nightly ritual—not a task, but a tether back to yourself.

Personal Reflection:
Reclaiming My Space, Reclaiming Myself

Before my stroke, I lived in constant motion, professor, therapist, mother, wife, healer.
I was a storm of service, a woman shaped by systems that measure worth in exhaustion.
I poured from every cup until mine ran dry.
The system had taught me that *worth was performance and care was currency.*

Then my body said, "no more."

My stroke became both rupture and revelation, my body's sacred disruption.
Not a betrayal, but a boundary. Not an ending, but an intervention.
It tore through illusion and demanded a new way of being, one that didn't center on what I could produce, but who I could become if I simply stopped.

In the days after, I remember lying still, terrified by the unfamiliar quiet of my own body.

Shame crept in—the kind that whispers, *you should be stronger than this.*

I had always been the one others leaned on. But now, I was the one trembling, the one asking for help.

I thought my body had failed me, but what I came to realize was this: my body wasn't failing, it was finally telling the truth.

One night, as tears traced the edges of my pillow, I heard a whisper rise from somewhere deep inside:

"Rest is not weakness. Rest is remembrance."

Those words became a mantra, a medicine, a map.

And that's when I began creating what is now my healing room—a sacred space where I could breathe without performing strength.

At first, it was just survival, a quiet corner to meditate and stretch.

But over time, it grew into something much bigger, a sanctuary that mirrors my spirit.

The room sits at the heart of my home, where the morning light spills gently through the window.

Candles line the shelves, some tall and white, some rich and golden, each one lit for a different intention: healing, clarity, forgiveness, peace.

Their flames flicker like small prayers, reminding me that even fire knows how to rest in its own rhythm.

Along the back wall stretches my library, a collection of books chosen not for research, but for joy.

Fiction and poetry. Stories written by Black women whose words remind me that softness is not surrender.

Each spine feels like a friend—Audre, Toni, Bell, Maya, Jennifer, Michelle—all standing shoulder to shoulder, keeping me company on the days when silence feels too heavy.

There's a small altar adorned with objects that root me in my BYRD roots:

- Belonging: A framed photo of my daughters and granddaughters, their laughter frozen mid-joy, reminding me that love is my lineage.

- Yielding: A smooth river stone I hold when I need to remember that stillness, too, is sacred movement.

- Resilience: Many carved elephants, unshaken, ancient, enduring.

- Disruption: A piece of kente cloth draped across my chair—bold, unapologetic, alive.

In this room, I am not Mrs. Byrd, not therapist, not mother, not professor, just Shar.

A woman rebuilding her rhythm.

A woman listening to her body's wisdom.

A woman remembering what it feels like to *belong to herself.*

Some days, I light the candles and simply breathe.

Other days, I dance, slow, intentional movements that remind my body she is still capable of grace.

Sometimes, I sit cross-legged on the floor, tracing the titles of books I haven't yet read, whispering thank you to the ancestors who carried me here.

And when grief rises, as it still does, I let it.

I cry.

I pray.

I listen.

My sister and best friend Talanda Donahue, better known as Sunshine, once told me something that has never left me:

"You deserve a space that reflects your sacredness."

Those words took root in me. They changed how I saw my environment, my work, my body.

I stopped asking for permission to slow down. I began tending to myself like sacred ground.

Now, when I step into that room, I am not escaping my life, I am

returning to it.
Each breath becomes a bridge back to belonging.
Each pause, a reclamation of my body's right to rest.
Each act of care—lighting a candle, turning a page, pouring tea—
becomes a sermon of self-remembrance.

This space is not just a room.
It is a revolution in four walls, a declaration that Black women deserve
rest without guilt, healing without proving, softness without explanation.
Here, I am not performing strength.
I am practicing freedom.
of my body's right to rest.

PART III:
THE NERVOUS
SYSTEM AS
WITNESS: BREATH,
OPPRESSION &
LIBERATION

Interlude
The ROOM that Remembers Me

I am the room that remembers you.
Before the stroke. Before the silence. Before the world taught your bones
to move faster than your soul could follow.

You built me from breath and heartbreak, from the slow gathering of
things that whispered,
"You deserve to be held, too."

I watched you enter, cautious at first
unsure if stillness could be trusted.
You lit one candle. Then another.
And the light bent toward you, as if it had been waiting.

The air here hums differently now.
It smells like sage and surrender.
The walls know your sighs by name.

Every book on the shelf has a pulse
stories of Black women who learned that softness was not surrender
but ceremony.
They lean against one another like sisters in a pew,
testifying quietly each time you reach for them.

The chair in the corner still holds your shape,
your spine slowly unclenching from the years of being "strong."
The floor has absorbed your prayers, your tears, your laughter
and sometimes, when the wind moves through the open window,

you can hear the echo of your ancestors' hands clapping softly
in approval.

You have filled me with the holy scent of resilience:
cocoa butter, candle wax, and the faint salt of release.
Each time you light a flame, you remind me, and yourself
that your fire was never lost, only waiting for breath.

You call me your healing room.
But really, beloved,
I am the one healed by you.

Because each time you step inside,
you teach me what sacred Black rest looks like.
You teach me how a body becomes its own altar.
You teach me that liberation hums in the rhythm of deep, unhurried
breathing.

And when you leave
to teach, to mother, to fight, to love
I keep your peace safe here.
Folded in the quiet.
Waiting for your return.

So come back to me, again and again,
not when the world breaks you,
but before it can.

Sit.
Breathe.
Be.

I am your mirror, your witness, your reminder.
You are not performing strength here.
You are practicing freedom.

And I, the room that remembers you
will hold that truth
until you remember it too.

Closing Blessing: The Body as Sacred Text

Place your hand on your heart and whisper:

"My body is my first home.
My breath is my inheritance.
My rest is my resistance.
My presence is my disruption."

Let that truth pulse through your bloodstream like prayer.
Because every time a Black woman slows her breath, softens her shoulders, and chooses peace over productivity,
she heals not only herself
she heals the lineage that walks behind her.

Chapter 25
Breath Awareness—
Activating the
Parasympathetic
Nervous System

The Breath as Liberation

Breath is the oldest language of the body.

It is the first sound we make when we enter this world and the last we release when we leave it.

But for Black bodies, breath has always been both sacred and political, an act of survival in systems designed to constrict, choke, and silence.

When I say *breathe,* I'm not speaking of oxygen alone; I'm speaking of remembrance.

I'm speaking of reclaiming what the world has tried to take from us: ease, rhythm, belonging, rest.

Breathing is our most accessible tool for nervous system regulation, yet under stress, many of us forget how to breathe fully and deeply.

Our bodies constrict; our ribs cage in. We hold our breath without realizing it, bracing against the world's weight.

Diaphragmatic breathing, or deep belly breathing, activates the vagus nerve, the great communicator of calm. It awakens the parasympathetic nervous system, guiding the body out of fight, flight, or freeze and into a state of restoration.

Try this: The BYRD Breath Sequence

A breath rooted in Belonging, Yielding, Resilience, and Disruption.

1. Inhale (Belonging) through your nose, matching your own unique breathing patterns.
    Let your belly rise. Whisper internally, *I am connected. I am seen.*

2. Hold (Yielding), for your comfort level.
    Feel the weight of gravity holding you.
    Let your shoulders soften. Let the ground carry some of your story.

3. Exhale (Resilience) through your mouth, matching your own unique breathing patterns.
    Let go of what is not yours to carry today—the hypervigilance, the people-pleasing, the proving.
    Say softly, *"I am healing."*

4. Pause (Disruption). Rest before the next inhale.
    This pause—this stillness—is an act of defiance.
    The system may demand that you rush, but your body chooses peace.

Repeat for several rounds.
With each cycle, imagine your breath widening the walls inside you that once held too much.

Relearning Safety Through the Body

During my stroke recovery, I had to retrain my body to move without fear, to trust that my nervous system still knew the way home.
There were moments when my body trembled at the thought of movement, when I feared the unknown terrain of recovery.

But then came the breath.
I would pause, close my eyes, and whisper:

Inhale, I am safe.
Exhale, I am healing.

That rhythm became my medicine.
The breath was not just air; it was memory.
A remembering that I could return to my body and not be betrayed.

Each breath carried the reminder:

Safety is not the absence of danger; it is the presence of connection.

Visualization: Anchoring in Safety

For many of us, true safety has never been guaranteed.
Our bodies remember the generational alarms, the tightening of muscles,
the vigilance in our ancestors' bones.
But the nervous system does not need perfection to regulate.
It needs *glimpses* of safety, moments where the body remembers what
calm feels like.

Try this: The Safer Space Visualization

Close your eyes and call to mind a place where you have felt held, seen,
and safer.
Maybe it's your grandmother's kitchen, filled with cornbread
and laughter.
Maybe it's a sunlit forest, or your church pew during a hymn that cracks
the soul open just enough to let light in.

When I visualize safety, I often return to that moment in Lake Tahoe.
After the cruelty, after the snowplow drenched our coats and dignity,
came compassion.
A white couple stopped. They wrapped us in blankets, helped my father
dig the car out, and stayed until we were warm.

Now, when my nervous system trembles, I don't anchor to the violence; I anchor to the kindness that followed.
To the warmth.
To the reminder that humanity can exist even in cold places.

I close my eyes and imagine the weight of that blanket, the softness of their concern, the relief in my father's shoulders.
And something in my body settles.

Safety, for me, is that blanket, the bridge between trauma and tenderness.

Connection with Others: Healing Through Relationship

The Polyvagal Theory teaches us that we regulate best not alone, but *together*.
Dr. Stephen Porges calls it *co-regulation*, the way our nervous systems borrow calm from one another through tone, gaze, breath, and presence.

Our ancestors already knew this.
Black and Brown bodies have always healed in community, through song, through rhythm, through prayer circles and porch laughter.
Regulation has always been relational.

Try this: The Breath of Belonging

When you feel overwhelmed, reach out.
Not necessarily to talk, but to be seen, to be held in the rhythm of someone else's peace.

During my recovery, there were nights when fear swallowed the room whole.
My breath would shorten, my body buzzed with anxiety.

But then came Minister Katrina Barnes, her voice soft yet commanding,

her prayers wrapping around me like a lullaby.
And Brother Chester "Chet" Hutchinson, whose calm strength filled
the space like an anchor in a storm. He didn't need to say much; his
stillness spoke safety. His presence reminded me that faith can be quiet
and solid, that sometimes, regulation comes not through words, but
through energy.

They prayed over me, not to fix, but to cover.
To remind my nervous system of what it had forgotten:

You are held.
You are seen.
You are safe.

Their presence was medicine.
Their faith, a form of co-regulation.
Each prayer lowered my heart rate; each hum deepened my breath.

This is what the Belonging Root in the BYRD Model teaches us
that safety lives in relationship, and healing often begins in the shared
exhale between souls who see one another.

Ancestral Practices: Breath as Ceremony

Our ancestors have always known the body's intelligence.
Long before we named the vagus nerve, they sang its language.
They rocked babies into regulation.
They hummed through pain and swayed through sorrow.

When we breathe with intention, we awaken that lineage—
we call forth the wisdom stored in our mitochondrial memory,
the quiet knowing that *we have been here before, and we survived.*

Try this: The Ancestral Breath Ritual

Light a candle.

Close your eyes.

Breathe deeply and imagine your ancestors standing in a circle around you.

With each inhale, feel their breath joining yours.

With each exhale, release the fear that does not belong to you.

I often return to the hymns my grandmother sang while she cooked. Sometimes I can still hear her voice, sweet and steady, the sound of safety long before I understood the science of regulation.

When I hum those hymns now, I feel her hand on my back, my breath syncing with hers across time.

This is the Resilience Root, the body remembering what it was built to endure, and the spirit remembering who it comes from.

The Sacred Disruption of Rest

Every time we breathe fully, we are disrupting a system that profits from our exhaustion.

The BYRD Model reminds us:

- Belonging connects us back to community.

- Yielding invites softness and surrender.

- Resilience reclaims our embodied strength.

- Disruption declares rest as rebellion.

When we breathe slowly, we reject the violence of urgency.

We say, *"I am not machinery. I am sacred flesh."*

We remind our bodies that safety is not earned through overperformance; it is our inheritance.

The BYRD Breath Ladder:
A Somatic Guide for Daily Regulation

"Every breath is a bridge, from the past to the present, from the body to the divine."

The BYRD Breath Ladder is not a technique; it's a practice of returning. Each step invites the nervous system into safety, the spirit into softness, and the mind into presence.
It honors what is both physiological and spiritual: the breath as medicine, the body as altar, and rest as resistance.

Each rung of this ladder corresponds to a root of your model, Belonging, Yielding, Resilience, and Disruption, and to the Four Roots Framework, Identity, Story, Body, and System.

1. Belonging—The Breath of Connection

(Identity Root: Remembering Who You Are)

Purpose:
To awaken safety through connection, to self, ancestors, and community.

Practice:

1. Sit or stand with your feet grounded.

2. Place your hand over your heart.

3. Inhale slowly through your nose for four counts, whispering:
   I belong here.

4. Exhale through your mouth for six counts, whispering:
   I am connected to something greater than this moment.

5. Imagine your ancestors standing in a circle around you—every inhale drawing in their strength, every exhale softening into their care.

Reflection Prompt:

Where does belonging live in my body today?
What relationships or communities remind me that I am not alone?

Nervous System Impact:
Activates the ventral vagal pathway, the "social safety system," calming the body through connection cues.

2. Yielding—The Breath of Surrender

(Story Root: Rewriting What Survival Taught You)

Purpose:
To invite softness into the body's defenses. Yielding is not collapse; it is conscious release.

Practice:

1. Inhale deeply, feeling your belly expand like a tide.

2. Hold for two counts, noticing where your body resists.

3. Exhale slowly and fully, saying softly:
   "I let go of the need to perform strength."

4. Allow your shoulders to drop. Let your jaw unclench.

5. Repeat for five rounds, inviting your breath to move lower into your belly with each cycle.

Ritual Variation:
Light a candle or anoint your palms with oil. As you exhale, visualize tension leaving your hands and rising into the flame.

Reflection Prompt:

What stories of overfunctioning or perfection am I ready to release?
Where can I yield without losing myself?

Nervous System Impact:
Engages the parasympathetic system through long exhales, signaling safety and allowing muscles to relax.

3. Resilience—The Breath of Reclamation

(Body Root: Reconnecting to the Wisdom Within)

Purpose:
To restore vitality and remind the body of its strength after rupture or fatigue.

Practice:

1. Stand tall or sit upright with both feet flat.

2. Inhale through your nose for four counts, arms rising overhead.

3. Hold for one beat—feel the fullness in your lungs.

4. Exhale powerfully through your mouth with an audible sigh.

5. With each exhale, imagine shaking loose the residue of stress—roll your shoulders, stretch your neck, sway your hips.

Reflection Prompt:

What strength am I carrying that I have not yet acknowledged?
How has my body kept me alive when my spirit felt too tired to try?

Ritual Variation:
Hum softly as you exhale; vibration through the chest stimulates the vagus nerve and regulates the heart rate.

Nervous System Impact:
Restores balance between the sympathetic (activation) and parasympathetic (rest) systems, fostering vitality without overwhelm.

4. Disruption—The Breath of Liberation

(System Root: Refusing Erasure and Choosing Expansion)

Purpose:
To reclaim agency and disrupt inherited narratives of smallness.
This is where rest becomes resistance, and stillness becomes strategy.

Practice:

1. Inhale deeply for five counts, lifting your chin slightly, as if greeting the horizon.

2. Hold the breath, feel the power coiling in your diaphragm.

3. Exhale through pursed lips, imagining your breath clearing the space around you.

4. Whisper aloud:
   "I am not small. I am sacred."

5. After each round, pause. Let silence stretch. Let your nervous system feel the steadiness of disruption.

Reflection Prompt:

What systems or beliefs have tried to constrict my breath?
What does freedom feel like in my body today?

Nervous System Impact:
Balances activation and grounding, empowering assertive calm rather than defensive tension.

Ritual Variation:
Play a drumbeat or tap your chest rhythmically as you breathe, honoring the ancestral pulse that says, "We are still here."

Integration Practice: The Full BYRD Cycle

At the end of your day, take ten minutes for the Full BYRD Breath.
Move through each phase like a ceremony:

1. Belonging: Inhale and remember, *I am connected.*

2. Yielding: Exhale what isn't yours to carry.

3. Resilience: Breathe strength into your spine.

4. Disruption: Rest your body as an act of rebellion.

Between each stage, pause. Listen. Let the breath write its own story through you.

When you finish, sit in silence.
Place your hand on your heart and whisper:

"I belong. I yield. I rise. I disrupt."

That is your nervous system's prayer of freedom.
That is your inheritance made breath.

Closing Reflection: Reclaiming Our Right to Regulate

Our breath is more than biology—it is resistance, remembrance,
and rebirth.
Every inhale is a reclamation.
Every exhale, a prayer.

To breathe deeply as a Black woman, as a BIPOC healer,
is to rewrite the story of survival through the body.
It is to say: *I belong to myself. I belong to this breath.*

When I breathe now, I imagine my daughters—each inhale a letter to them,
each exhale a blessing:

You are allowed to rest.
You are allowed to heal.
You are allowed to take up space.

Nervous system regulation is not a privilege; it is a right.
It is our birthright to feel safe in our bodies, to breathe without apology,
to live without bracing.

When we reclaim the breath, we reclaim the lineage.
When we regulate, we resist.
When we rest, we rise.

Chapter 26
How the Nervous System Responds to Systemic Oppression and Bias

(The Body's Long Memory and the Breath of Liberation)

Our bodies are the first to know when something is not right. Long before words form or thoughts take shape, the body remembers, contracts, tightens, and guards. For Black bodies, this is not a temporary response; it is an inherited state.

Systemic oppression is not an abstract idea; it is a physiological imprint. It alters our breathing, quickens our pulse, and teaches our muscles to live on high alert. It shapes posture, tone, and even digestion, the unseen choreography of surviving in a world that does not always welcome us.

Western medicine calls it chronic stress activation.
I call it the body's testimony.

Every time we swallow our truth to stay employed, every time we smile to soften someone else's fear, every time we shrink to survive a room not meant for our fullness, our nervous system writes it down.
Line by line. Cell by cell.
The body keeps the minutes of injustice.

The BYRD Model as Nervous System Map

Each pillar of the BYRD Model offers a different pathway for our bodies to remember safety in the midst of harm:

- Belonging: The antidote to systemic isolation. When the world says *you don't fit,* the body whispers, *you still belong.*

- Yielding: The invitation to rest when vigilance has become religion.

- Resilience: The muscle memory of our ancestors who kept breathing under impossible weight.

- Disruption: The sacred rebellion of saying *no more*—to both oppression and the self-erasure it demands.

Through this lens, healing racialized trauma is not just emotional recovery; it's nervous system reclamation.

Microaggressions and the Fight-or-Flight Response

(System Root—Survival as an Everyday Praxis)

Microaggressions are not subtle; they are sanctioned wounds dressed as feedback.
They arrive in emails, in meetings, in evaluations that twist truth into performance notes.
And the body feels each one like a bruise beneath the skin.

I remember reading my annual evaluation, my eyes catching on a line that stopped my breath cold:

"Demonstrates limited understanding."

Limited.

That single word lodged itself in my throat.
It wasn't just untrue, it was dishonest, a quiet attempt to rewrite my competence.

My body reacted before my mind could reason with it: a flush of heat across my chest, a tightening in my jaw, my pulse quickening into defense.

This is how the sympathetic nervous system answers injustice.
Fight or flight.
Rage or retreat.

But in systems where truth is punished and silence is rewarded, neither feels safe.
Fighting risks the labels *angry, emotional, unprofessional.*
Yielding feels like betrayal of self.
So the body learns to brace.

I smiled through the sting.
I wrote my rebuttal carefully, every sentence measured, every emotion trimmed.
But inside, my nervous system screamed for acknowledgment.

Each restrained response became cortisol in my bloodstream.
Each breath I held became proof of how deeply my professionalism had been weaponized against me.
Each dishonest line in that evaluation became another entry in the body's long archive of systemic gaslighting.

This is what living in constant activation feels like
the body's quiet rebellion against erasure,
the nervous system's testimony that the harm is real.

And yet, beneath the trembling, something ancestral stirred, my Belonging Root speaking through the constriction:

"You are not limited. You are luminous."

That whisper became my anchor.
That truth became my pulse.

Because even as the system tried to shrink me into its narrative, my body

refused to forget who I was
a woman whose understanding is not limited but limitless, born from
generations who survived, learned, and kept creating wisdom out
of wounds.

Exclusion and the Freeze/Shutdown Response

(Body Root—When Stillness is Survival)

Not all trauma screams. Some of it whispers, *stay small.*
Some of it freezes the voice in the throat and turns fire into fog.

The freeze response is not weakness. It is the body's mercy—the sacred
pause that says, *if escape is impossible, conserve energy.*

When we are continually overlooked, interrupted, or ignored, our nervous
system learns: "Speaking doesn't help. Silence keeps you safe."

I've watched colleagues grow dimmer over time, their light folding
inward. Brilliant Black and Brown clinicians once alive with vision now
speaking softly, cautiously, calculating every sentence before it leaves
their lips.
Their passion hadn't died; it had simply gone underground, buried
beneath the weight of *professional composure.*

The world calls it burnout.
But I know it as the freeze of accumulated harm, the body's reluctant
agreement to survive without thriving.

This is what Yielding in distortion looks like: the surrender that comes
from exhaustion, not peace.
But when we reclaim Yielding as sacred rest, we begin to thaw.
We begin to remember that stillness can be chosen, not forced.

Being Labeled an "Angry Black Woman"

(Identity Root—The Politics of Emotional Containment)

There is a special violence reserved for Black women's truth—the way it gets reinterpreted, repackaged, and rejected.

If we speak up, we are *too aggressive.*
If we stay silent, we are *too passive.*
If we cry, we are *too fragile.*
If we stay calm, we are *too detached.*

Our emotional range is policed more than our performance is praised.
And yet, our nervous systems keep trying to find safety in a world that confuses our passion with danger.

I remember a meeting where I calmly raised the lack of cultural representation in leadership. My tone was grounded; my data was solid.
A white supervisor looked at me and said,

"Maybe if you weren't so emotional about it, people would listen."

Emotional?
What they really meant was: *You made me uncomfortable.*

In that moment, my body felt the electric surge of fight-or-flight again.
My pulse raced, but my professionalism demanded stillness.
So I stayed quiet, but the silence was not peace; it was paralysis.

For days after, I felt the residue, the jaw pain, the fatigue, the insomnia.
My body was doing the work of holding what the system refused to acknowledge.

This is the Belonging wound: to be in the room but never truly seen.
To be visible yet invisible, competent yet questioned, powerful yet contained.

The Epigenetics of Oppression

(Story Root—The Science of Inherited Vigilance)

Trauma doesn't start with us; it travels through us.

Epigenetics teaches us that chronic stress alters gene expression, not the genes themselves, but how they *speak*. Methylation marks can silence certain protective pathways and amplify the ones wired for survival.

Western science calls this gene modulation.
Our ancestors called it memory in the blood.

When our grandmothers held their breath to stay alive, their bodies sent a message to ours: *Be ready. Stay alert. Don't relax too soon.*
When our fathers bowed their heads in humility to survive humiliation, their nervous systems rehearsed restraint so that ours would inherit control.

We are the descendants of brilliance disguised as endurance.
But what was once protection can become imprisonment.

Healing means rewriting the code, sending new messages down the bloodline:

"You can exhale now."
"You are safe enough to soften."
"You can rest."

That is the Resilience Root, not just surviving the storm, but teaching our DNA that the storm has passed.

The Somatic Toll of Silence

(System Root—When the Body Speaks What the System Denies)

I've lost count of the times I've been told to "be careful," as if my truth were a weapon rather than a contribution.
Each warning felt like another microdose of fear injected into my nervous system.
It's no wonder so many of us wake up tired after a day of doing "nothing wrong."

Because we didn't just attend a meeting, we *managed our tone, translated our thoughts, tracked our microexpressions, and performed safety* for others who never had to earn it.

That's not fatigue; that's somatic taxation.
That's the price of being "the only one in the room."

When I left that meeting, my jaw ached from clenching. My breath was shallow, my heart racing, my body heavy.
The next morning, I wasn't simply exhausted; I was neurologically depleted.

And yet, even in that depletion, something ancient stirred—the knowing that we have survived worse, and that our bodies, though tired, still hold the blueprint for repair.

This is where Disruption begins, not in rage, but in reclamation.
Disruption says:

"My nervous system deserves peace."
"My body will not be a casualty of your comfort."
"I will rest even when the system says I haven't earned it."

Collective Regulation: Healing in Communion

After my stroke, it was not medicine alone that healed me; it was community.
It was people like Minister Katrina, who prayed life into the spaces my fear had silenced.
It was Brother Chet, whose quiet steadiness became a living example of regulated presence, a reminder that peace can be embodied, not just spoken.
Their calm nervous systems lent rhythm to mine until I could breathe again on my own.

This is the power of co-regulation, the nervous system's way of remembering safety through others.
When one of us breathes deeply, we invite the room to breathe with us.

That is the work.
That is liberation, one nervous system at a time.

BYRD Nervous System Reflection Practice

(A Somatic Map for Reclaiming Safety in an Unsafe World)

"The body does not forget, but it does forgive, when we finally listen."

This reflection practice is not an assignment. It's an altar.
A sacred moment to sit with your body, not as a problem to fix, but as a witness to honor.

You will move through each pillar of the BYRD Model, Belonging, Yielding, Resilience, and Disruption, using the Four Roots Framework—Identity, Story, Body, and System—as your map.
Go slowly.
Breathe between each prompt.
Let your body lead.

1. Belonging—Finding Safety in Connection

(Identity Root—Remembering Who You Are)

Take a breath and place your hand over your heart.
Feel your pulse—the quiet drumbeat of an unbroken lineage.

Reflection Prompts:

- Where in my body do I feel disconnected from safety?
- Who or what helps me remember that I am not alone?
- When was the last time I felt truly seen, not for what I produce, but for who I am?

Somatic Practice:

- Lean your back against a wall or chair. Feel its support.
- Whisper aloud: *I am supported. I am rooted. I belong.*

Body Wisdom:

- Notice how your spine lengthens when you remember belonging.
- That's your nervous system trusting gravity again.

2. Yielding—Resting Without Permission

(Story Root—Rewriting the Narrative of Endurance)

So many of us were raised on the gospel of overfunctioning.
We were told rest was lazy. But the body knows better.
It knows that slowing down is how we return to rhythm.

Reflection Prompts:

- Where do I still confuse exhaustion with purpose?
- What stories about rest or worth do I need to release?
- How does my body ask for rest, and how do I usually respond?

Somatic Practice:

- Inhale deeply through your nose.
- Exhale through your mouth with a sigh.
- Allow your shoulders to drop.
- Repeat three times.
- Now say softly: *I yield not to weakness, but to wisdom.*

Body Wisdom:

- When your muscles unclench, your story begins to rewrite itself.
- Yielding is the body's language for trust.

3. Resilience—Remembering the Body's Strength

(Body Root—Honoring Survival Without Glorifying Suffering)

Our bodies are not broken; they are brilliant.
Every adaptation, every tremor, every tear has been a way to keep us alive.
Resilience is not perfection. It's persistence with purpose.

Reflection Prompts:

- Where in my body do I feel strength right now, even if it's small?
- How has my body protected me in ways I didn't recognize before?
- What inherited strength still lives in my cells?

Somatic Practice:

- Stand up tall.
- Press your feet firmly into the ground.
- Place your hand over your heart and whisper: *I survived. I am still becoming.*

Now take three grounding breaths.

Feel how the earth steadies you from beneath, like an ancestor you never met but somehow remember.

Body Wisdom:

- Resilience is not about holding everything, it's about knowing when to let go.

- It's the exhale after centuries of holding your breath.

4. Disruption—Choosing Liberation Through the Body

(System Root—Rest as Rebellion, Breath as Boundary)

Disruption is the sacred art of saying *no* to what harms and *yes* to what heals.
It is the body refusing to perform safety for systems that are unsafe.

Reflection Prompts:

- Where in my body do I still hold someone else's comfort above my own peace?

- What systems or relationships teach my body to shrink?

- How can I make rest and truth part of my resistance?

Somatic Practice:

- Inhale through your nose for four counts.

- Hold your breath for two.

- Exhale slowly for six, whispering: *I am not small. I am sacred.*

Imagine your breath as a wave clearing old residue from your cells.
Let your exhale stretch into silence.

Body Wisdom:

- Disruption doesn't always look loud; sometimes it's a deep breath you refuse to apologize for.

Integration: Writing Safety into Your Story

As you complete this reflection, pause and notice—what has shifted?
Your heart rate? Your posture? Your breath?
This is your nervous system remembering it can move again.

Take a pen and write:

"My body is not my enemy. It is my elder, my witness, and my home."

You might also add your own affirmation, something alive in this moment:

- "I am safe enough to rest."

- "My ancestors breathe through me."

- "I am building a new nervous system for the generations to come."

Closing Reflection:
The BYRD Breath of Liberation

1. Inhale: "I belong."

2. Hold: "I yield."

3. Exhale: "I rise."

4. Pause: "I disrupt."

Repeat three times.
On the final exhale, whisper your name like a prayer, a reclamation of everything the system tried to forget.

Then rest your hand over your heart and feel it
the steady, undeniable rhythm of survival turned to song.

That is your nervous system healing.
That is your freedom work, happening in real time.

CHAPTER 27
THE COST OF
SHRINKING OURSELVES

(System Root—When Silence Becomes Survival)

There comes a moment when the weight of shrinking ourselves becomes heavier than the risk of being heard. Shrinking is the nervous system's way of negotiating with systems that confuse our truth for threat.

Silence settles into the bones, disguising itself as peace, but the body knows better.

The nervous system records every betrayal of self, each time we swallow truth, each time we dim our light to protect someone else's comfort.

For years, I believed endurance was power. I thought composure was grace.

But beneath the stillness, my body was screaming.

The tension in my shoulders. The knot in my stomach. The shallow breath that never seemed to fill my lungs.

These weren't random discomforts, they were messages, the body's alarm bells saying:

"You are abandoning yourself to make them comfortable."

And that kind of betrayal has a cost.

A cost measured not in moments, but in years.

In headaches that never fade.

In confidence that quietly erodes.

In the slow disappearance of one's own voice.

Reclaiming My Voice and My Nervous System

(Body Root—Listening to the Wisdom Beneath the Skin)

After I read the evaluation that falsely claimed I had "limited understanding," something in me cracked open.

I realized I could not control the narratives written about me, but I could control the way I honored my own truth.

The body, after all, is not only where we hold trauma.
It is where liberation begins.

So, I began practicing Somatic Liberation, guided by the BYRD Model: Belonging, Yielding, Resilience, and Disruption.

Belonging reminded me that my understanding was not limited, it was rooted.
Rooted in culture, in experience, in a lineage of wisdom that no evaluation could quantify.

Yielding taught me that rest was not surrender, but strategy.
That slowing down was a sacred act of resistance in a system that feeds on our exhaustion.

Resilience became the pulse in my chest, the reminder that survival had never been the goal. Wholeness was.

And Disruption, my favorite root, taught me that healing sometimes looks like speaking the truth even when your voice shakes.

I began to regulate my nervous system not as a self-care trend, but as an act of remembrance.

My practices became prayers:

- Placing my hand over my heart and feeling the beat of belonging.

- Breathing deeply, letting each exhale whisper: *I am safe enough to be seen.*

- Reframing my inner narrative: *I am not too passionate. I am precise. I am purpose embodied.*

- Noticing where I held tension, in the jaw, in the belly, in the breath, and releasing it like smoke from ancestral fire.

Each time I listened to my body instead of silencing it, I reclaimed a piece of myself that the system had tried to steal.

Moving Forward: A Lesson in Liberation

(Story Root—Rewriting What Survival Means)

I wish I could say it never happened again, the gaslighting, the subtle erasure, the professional violence that comes dressed in civility.
But the truth is, systems built on oppression don't dissolve when you find your voice.
They double down.

What changed wasn't the system.
What changed was me.

I stopped mistaking passion for a flaw.
I stopped apologizing for taking up space.
I stopped translating my truth into a language palatable to fragility.

And in that transformation, I began to live differently.

I think often of my daughters, brilliant, bold, Black women rising in a world that still asks them to dim.
I don't want them to inherit the exhaustion of my silence.
I want them to inherit the rhythm of my breath, steady, unapologetic, free.

So, I keep speaking.

I keep breathing.
I keep honoring the wisdom in my body, even when the world doesn't.

Because true healing doesn't come from being careful.
It comes from being whole.

Practices for Navigating Systemic Stress

(Integration of All Four Roots)

Systemic oppression doesn't just bruise the psyche, it imprints
on the body.
Our nervous systems absorb centuries of fear and adaptation.
We flinch at tones that sound like danger.
We brace at meetings that echo old hierarchies.
We learn to survive by contracting, not expanding.

But through Belonging, Yielding, Resilience, and Disruption, we can
begin to rewrite the story of our bodies.

1. Naming the Harm

(Identity Root—Speaking What Was Silenced)

Oppression disguises itself as professionalism, as evaluation, as "constructive feedback."
But the body knows the difference.

When your stomach twists before a meeting...
When your breath shortens before you speak truth...
When fatigue settles in after being ignored...

That's your body calling out injustice in real time.
Name it. Speak it. Write it down.
Each acknowledgment reclaims ownership of your narrative.

2. Grounding Through the Senses

(Body Root—Safety in the Present)

When the system pulls you into survival, return to your body.
Touch something real. Feel something solid.

- Press your feet into the ground and whisper, *I belong here.*

- Run your fingers over a grounding object—a smooth stone, a ring, a pendant that carries memory.

- Inhale the scent of something soothing—lavender, sandalwood, or the familiar spice of your kitchen.

Each sensory anchor reminds your nervous system that the threat is not now, that you are safe enough to breathe.

3. Advocating with Support

(System Root—Collective Regulation as Resistance)

We were never meant to do this alone.
Advocacy without community becomes martyrdom.

Find your people, the ones who will echo your truth in rooms that try to silence it.
Stand together, speak together, rest together.

Collective regulation is not only strategy; it is medicine.
When one of us breathes deeply, the others remember how.

4. Connecting to Ancestral Strength

(Story Root—Remembering Who Carries You)

When you feel small, remember whose breath you are borrowing.
Imagine the hands of those who came before, steady on your shoulders.

Hear them whisper:

"You come from endurance that became art."
"You come from resilience that learned to rest."

Your healing is not only for you; it is a continuation of theirs.
Every time you choose rest, you are undoing a wound they were
forced to bear.

The Impact on Clinicians:
Holding Space While Carrying Weight

(Belonging & System Roots—Reclaiming the Right to Be Held)

For Black clinicians, and all BIPOC healers, this dual existence is
relentless.
We hold the trauma of others while carrying our own.
We facilitate regulation in systems that dysregulate us.
We create safe spaces for clients in institutions that remain unsafe for us.

This is not weakness.
This is the cost of caring in a system designed to forget our humanity.

But we are remembering.
And remembrance is rebellion.

So we build spaces that hold us back.
We breathe together, pray together, cry together.
Because healing is not a solo act, it is a collective return to wholeness.

Personal Reflection:
When the Body Speaks, We Must Listen

(Resilience Root—The Moment of Return)

Lying in my hospital bed after my stroke, I had no choice but to listen. No emails. No meetings. No demands. Just me and the truth my body had been whispering for years.

It had been speaking in tension.
It had been speaking in headaches.
It had been speaking in exhaustion so deep it blurred into numbness.

And I, like so many of us, had called it normal.
I had named survival "strength."

But that day, my body said: enough.
Enough carrying the weight of injustice in silence.
Enough mistaking productivity for purpose.
Enough betraying my own nervous system for belonging.

That rupture became revelation.
That stillness became prayer.

Because when the body finally speaks, and we choose to listen, healing begins not as an idea, but as an embodied truth:

"I am no longer shrinking to fit this world. This world must expand to hold me."

Chapter 28
A Wake-Up Call
Wrapped in Love

(Belonging Root—Remembering That the Body Is Sacred Ground)

This was the beginning of my expansion, the moment I re-entered my body and refused to shrink ever again. During my recovery, my sister Sunshine and my best friend France took turns sitting by my bedside. Their presence was medicine, quiet, steady, grounding.

Even in the beeping and buzzing of hospital machinery, their laughter created a rhythm my nervous system could follow home.

Sunshine leaned close one night, her voice full of both tenderness and urgency.

"Your body is sacred," she said, shaking her head. "Girl, don't let these people kill you. Listen to its wisdom."

And then, we laughed.
Because sometimes truth lands so hard it knocks the wind out of you, and laughter is the only breath left.

Underneath that laughter lived a truth so deep it demanded transformation.
Her words weren't just advice, they were a *summons*.
A call back to myself.

I realized I had been breaking myself to fit into spaces that were never built to hold me.
Bending my body to meet impossible demands.

Sacrificing softness to survive professionalism.
Calling exhaustion "purpose" and collapse "dedication."

But that night, her words settled in my chest like a psalm:

My body is not an inconvenience to be pushed past; it is a guide.
It is wise. It knows when to rest, when to care, when to step away.
And if I refuse to listen, it will make me listen.

The Cost of Ignoring the Body's Wisdom

(System Root—When Survival Becomes the Standard)

I thought back to all the times I had overridden my body's voice:

- The knots in my stomach I called "stress," not warning.

- The shallow breaths I took in meetings where I didn't feel safe.

- The migraines that were really messages from my nervous system begging for stillness.

Each ignored signal was a betrayal of belonging.
Each dismissal was a denial of sacred knowing.

My stroke was not just a medical event; it was a reckoning.
A disruption.
A sacred intervention that said, *no more pretending wellness while dying inside.*

Relearning My Body's Language

(Body Root—The Return to Somatic Listening)

In the months that followed, I made a vow:
I would *listen.*

Listen not for pathology, but for wisdom.
Listen to the tightness, the tremors, the fatigue, as language.

That meant:

- Pausing before saying *yes* when my spirit whispered *no.*
- Tracing the tension in my body like a map of unspoken boundaries.
- Resting before collapse.
- Letting myself cry without apology.

And most importantly—
releasing the colonial myth that care must be *earned.*

I remember Sunshine's words like gospel:

"Don't let these people kill you."

And I realized—
so many of us are dying slowly, one dismissed boundary at a time.
One silenced truth at a time.
One act of self-abandonment at a time.

Our liberation begins the moment we decide that care is not a reward; it
is a right.

A Message for Anyone Who Needs It

(Story Root—Transforming Survival Into Legacy)

If you are reading this, pushing yourself to the brink—
waiting for the work to end,
the semester to finish,
the world to change—
before you rest...

I want you to hear me clearly:
Later is too late.

The body does not wait forever.
It whispers, then speaks, then screams.
And when we do not listen, it will demand stillness by force.

So listen.
Listen before your body has to make you.
Listen when your breath shortens, when your shoulders tighten,
when your spirit feels heavy for no reason at all.

Your body is not the enemy; it is the altar.
It is how your ancestors speak to you.
It is how your nervous system prays.

You deserve to be here, not just surviving, but whole.
Your healing does not have to wait.

Practices to Recognize and Regulate Nervous System Responses

(Integration—The BYRD Model in Motion)

Healing begins with awareness, with remembering the language
of the body.
For those of us shaped by systems that demanded we outperform, over-
give, and overlook ourselves,
awareness itself becomes an act of Disruption—
a refusal to participate in self-abandonment disguised as excellence.

Each time we tune in, we activate the Belonging Root—
reminding our nervous system that we are safe in our own skin.

Each time we slow down, we enter Yielding—
the sacred pause that allows restoration to flow through the body.

Each breath that expands without apology is Resilience—
evidence that we can survive without self-erasure.

And the decision to listen, to rest, to re-root—
that is Disruption—
the revolution of reclaiming one's life force.

Step 1: Recognizing Nervous System States

(Body Root—Reading the Signals of Safety and Stress)

Fight-or-Flight—The Gas Pedal (Sympathetic Activation)

- Physical Signs: racing heart, tight shoulders, clenched jaw.
- Emotional Signs: irritability, anxiety, urgency.

- Cognitive Signs: racing thoughts, difficulty focusing, feeling like you must always "do more."

Personal Reflection:
Before my stroke, I lived in fight mode.
Always producing, performing, protecting.
I mistook activation for passion, but my body was burning out.

Freeze—The Brake (Dorsal Vagal Shutdown)

When fight and flight fail, the body freezes to survive.

- Physical Signs: heavy limbs, fatigue, numbness.

- Emotional Signs: disconnection, hopelessness.

- Cognitive Signs: fog, indecision, feeling detached from yourself.

Personal Reflection:
After my stroke, I slipped into shutdown.
My body moved through recovery, but my spirit lagged behind.
I had to relearn that numbness is not peace; it's protection.

Safety & Connection—The Balance (Ventral Vagal Regulation)

This is the state of belonging, where the body rests, connects, and creates.

- Physical Signs: deep breathing, steady heart, relaxed muscles.

- Emotional Signs: contentment, openness.

- Cognitive Signs: clarity, curiosity, engagement.

Personal Reflection:
It took intentional stillness to rediscover this state—
slow mornings, prayer, laughter with my daughters,
the music of healing in ordinary moments.

Step 2: Regulating the Nervous System

(Resilience Root—Somatic Practices for Repair)

1. Grounding Through Sensation
Press your feet into the earth and whisper: *I am supported.*
Run your hands along something textured—wood, cloth, stone; feel
yourself return.

2. Breathwork for Belonging
Inhale through your nose for four counts, hold for two, exhale for six.
Let your exhale carry the weight that never belonged to you.

3. Visualization of Safety
Imagine your safe place—your grandmother's kitchen, your healing
room, your church pew, your sacred ocean.
The nervous system doesn't need proof; it only needs permission to
feel held.

4. Calling on Ancestral Strength
Light a candle. Say their names.
Feel the chorus of those who came before you breathing with you—
your lineage of resilience embodied.

5. Vagus Nerve Activation
Hum. Sing. Stretch the neck gently.
Feel vibration as prayer, breath as medicine.

6. Somatic Titration—Healing in Small Doses
Notice one sensation at a time.
Move between discomfort and ease like a wave.
Healing is not all at once; it is in rhythm with the body's pace.

Step 3: Building Daily Resilience Practices

(System & Story Roots—Healing as a Way of Life)

- Morning Grounding: Begin with breath or gratitude.

- Midday Reset: Step outside, stretch, touch sunlight.

- Evening Reflection: Journal your body's messages, not just your mind's thoughts.

Personal Reflection:

During my recovery, I'd sit with my daughters, our arms wrapped around each other.

The rhythm of rocking, the warmth of their bodies, that was my nervous system remembering safety.

That was belonging reborn.

A Final Reflection: The Revolution of Listening

(Disruption Root—When Healing Becomes Resistance)

Before my stroke, I called exhaustion normal.

I named suffering "strength."

But now, I know better.

Now, I listen.

I listen when my breath shortens, that's my body's plea for pause.

I listen when my shoulders ache, that's my spirit carrying what it was never meant to hold.

I listen when my fatigue lingers, that's my system saying, *belong to yourself again.*

To every healer, teacher, mother, clinician, and warrior reading this:

You do not need to earn your rest.

You do not need to apologize for your limits.

You do not need to break to be believed.

Because your body is sacred.
Your nervous system is an archive of survival, and a map to liberation.
Your healing is not indulgence; it is inheritance.
It belongs not just to you, but to everyone who comes after you.

So breathe.
And listen.
Because the revolution begins in the body that refuses to shrink anymore.

CHAPTER 29
THE POWER OF BREATH: USING BREATHWORK FOR HEALING AND GROUNDING

(Body Root—Breath as Bridge Between Worlds)

Opening Reflection: The Breath as Medicine and Mirror

Breath is both ancient and intimate.
It is the first sound we make entering this world, and the last we offer when we leave.
It is the soft pulse between chaos and calm, the language of the nervous system, the translator between body and soul.

Yet for so many of us, especially those carrying trauma, grief, or chronic stress, breath has become a battleground.
Each inhale feels heavy. Each exhale, hurried.
We forget that breathing was once effortless, a rhythm as natural as our heartbeat.

But breath remembers us even when we forget it.
It waits, patient, forgiving, until we are ready to return.

The Valley: When Breath Becomes a Battleground

(Yielding Root—Confronting the Body's Truth)

I have guided countless clients through breathwork. I could quote the research, describe the vagus nerve pathways, explain the soothing science of slow exhales.
But when it came to my own breath, I could not find refuge.

After my stroke, machines measured what I had ignored for years. My oxygen levels dipped low, my chest rose unevenly.
A sleep study revealed the truth: I stopped breathing in my sleep. Again and again.

The irony wasn't lost on me—a trauma therapist who taught breath as medicine was, herself, suffocating in her rest.
My breath had not failed me; I had failed to listen.

That revelation humbled me.
It stripped away everything I thought I knew about "control" and invited me into a deeper truth:
breathwork is not about *mastery*. It is about *relationship*.

The Rise: Reclaiming Breath on My Terms

(Resilience Root—Listening for the Body's Rhythm)

When I began again, I didn't count seconds. I didn't force expansion.
I simply listened.

Some days, my breath came in broken rhythms, like grief.
Other days, it arrived soft and full, like grace.
I learned to meet it where it was.

Breath became a quiet teacher:

- A sigh when I needed release.

- A hum when I needed grounding.

- A pause when I needed permission to stop performing.

I started walking to the rhythm of my own inhale and exhale, letting movement guide regulation.

No script, no structure, just reverence.

When I taught breathwork again, I no longer said, "take a deep breath." I said, "Find your breath."

Because breath is not a command, it's a conversation.

The Science and Soul of Breathwork

(System Root—The Nervous System as Sacred Design)

Breath is the only function of the autonomic nervous system we can consciously influence.

Every inhale is a conversation with the sympathetic system, the "gas pedal" of the body.

Every exhale whispers to the parasympathetic system, the "brake" that restores peace.

When we breathe shallowly, our body interprets danger.

When we breathe deeply and slowly, it signals safety, activating the ventral vagal nerve, our biological anchor of connection and calm.

But here's the truth trauma teaches: safety cannot be forced.

If the body has learned that stillness equals danger, deep breathing can feel like suffocation.

For trauma survivors, "relaxation" can actually trigger anxiety.

So breathwork must be approached not as a rule, but as a relationship. We listen before we lead. We attune before we adjust.

The Commitment: Breath as a Gentle Invitation

(Belonging Root—Creating Safety in the Self)

Now, when I guide breathwork, I invite curiosity instead of correction.
I ask:

- What kind of breath feels *safe* today?
- Does your body want to move while breathing, or be still?
- Can you let your breath come to you rather than chasing it?

This approach is radical in its softness.
It honors the intelligence of the body, a wisdom colonized systems
often deny.
Breathwork becomes less about "doing it right" and more about "being
with what is."

As I reclaimed my breath, I reclaimed belonging in my own body.
It was not about fixing; it was about coming home.

The Science and Benefits of Breathwork for Stress and Trauma

(Body Root Expanded)

The Breath–Nervous System Bridge

Our breath mirrors our inner world.
When anxious—shallow.
When grieving—held.
When grounded—flowing.

It is both mirror and medicine.
Through breath, we can shift the nervous system from chaos to calm,
from vigilance to vitality.

But only if we listen first.

The Breath–Stress Loop

Under threat, the sympathetic system takes the lead; breath becomes rapid, shallow, urgent.
Chronic stress keeps this system overactive, trapping us in perpetual readiness.
Intentional, gentle breathing reawakens the parasympathetic system, restoring balance and flexibility.

Our bodies need to feel safe before they can truly heal.
So we do not impose calm; we *invite* it.

When Breathwork Harms Instead of Heals

For survivors, especially those navigating racial trauma or medical mistrust, rigid techniques can feel oppressive.
"Take a deep breath" can sound like another demand from a world that already takes too much.
Our work, then, is not to prescribe, but to partner with the body, to follow its pace.

Chapter 30
Practical Breathwork Practices for Healing and Grounding

(Integration of All Four BYRD Roots)

Each of the following practices aligns with a BYRD pillar, inviting connection, rest, resilience, and disruption through the body's most sacred rhythm: breath.

1. Awareness-Based Breathing *(Belonging)*

Simply notice.
Don't change, don't correct.
Notice where your breath lives—chest, belly, throat.
Notice if it hides, or hums, or hesitates.
Your only task: witness.

Mantra: "My breath belongs to me."

2. Diaphragmatic Breathing *(Yielding)*

Place one hand on your belly, one on your chest.
Inhale slowly through your nose, letting your belly rise.

Exhale through your mouth, letting it fall.
Repeat gently, without striving.

Mantra: "I yield to the wisdom beneath my skin."

3. Extended Exhale Breathing *(Resilience)*

Breathe in for four counts, out for six.
Imagine exhaling the day's weight.
Each long exhale is a small rebellion, proof that rest can coexist with strength.

Mantra: "My rest is resistance."

4. Humming Breath *(Belonging + Ancestry)*

Inhale softly. Exhale with a hum.
Feel the vibration in your chest and jaw.
Let it echo like your grandmother's hymn, sound as survival.

Mantra: "I vibrate with the songs of those who came before me."

5. Gentle Breath with Movement *(Disruption)*

Stand or sit.
Inhale as you raise your arms or sway.
Exhale as you release.
Let your breath choreograph your healing.

Mantra: "Movement is my medicine."

Personal Reflection: Breath as Reclamation

Breathwork taught me what medicine could not: that healing is not compliance; it is relationship.
It taught me that my breath carries both inheritance and innovation—the breath of my ancestors, and the breath of a woman reclaiming her rhythm after rupture.

As I write this now, I breathe more slowly.
Not perfectly. Not evenly. But wholly.
Every inhale is a promise. Every exhale, a prayer.

I often remind my clients, and myself, that the body is our first home. When we tend to it gently, consistently, reverently, it becomes a space of liberation rather than a battleground. And to that I add: your breath is the doorway back home.

Chapter 31
Integrating Breathwork into Daily Life to Manage Compassion Fatigue

(BYRD Model woven throughout—Body/Belonging, Yielding, Resilience, Disruption; Roots: Story, Somatic, System, Sacred)

When Holding Space Becomes Too Heavy

Compassion fatigue is erosion by a thousand asks. It doesn't crash; it accumulates, especially for Black clinicians whose bodies absorb double labor: the clinical load and the racialized weather of the room. We hold stories in our tissues, swallow microaggressions between sessions, and call it "professionalism" while our breath grows thin.

I tried to outwork it, until my body said no. My stroke was a boundary my nervous system drew in permanent ink. Breathwork became a bridge back to myself, not performance, not perfection. Presence.

Daily Breathwork Practices for Healing

No special gear. No extra hour. Just rhythm and return.

1. Morning Grounding: Set the Weather (2–5 minutes)

BYRD = Belonging | Root = Somatic + Sacred

- Sit in your healing room—candles low, elephants watching like elders, your joy-only library within reach.
- One hand to heart, one to belly. Inhale through the nose, exhale through pursed lips.
- Whisper: *I am here. I am grounded. I am enough.*
- Optional: light a candle for an ancestor; let the first breath honor the ones who breathed before you.

Why it helps: You claim your breath before the day claims you.

2. Between-Session Reset: Release What Isn't Yours (60–120 seconds)

BYRD = Yielding | Root = System + Somatic

- Step to a doorway, window, or hallway.
- Inhale naturally; exhale longer than the inhale (no counting needed).
- On each exhale, name what you're releasing: *"Their fear out... their grief out... their rage out..."*
- Quick body sweep: unclench jaw, drop shoulders, soften belly.

Why it helps: The long exhale cues the parasympathetic system and signals to your body that you do not have to carry what you just witnessed.

3. Threshold Ritual: Transition From Doing to Being (3 minutes)

BYRD = Resilience | Root = Story + Sacred

- Before you leave your workspace or step through your front door:
    - Inhale while raising arms (or gently arching chest).
    - Exhale as arms float down. Three slow cycles.
    - Murmur: *"Work stays here. Love goes home."*
    - If emotions linger, add a humming exhale—low, steady, chesty.

Why it helps: Your body learns that endings are safe and repeatable.

4. The Voo Breath for Heavy Days (2–4 minutes)

BYRD = Disruption | Root = Somatic + Sacred

- Inhale softly. Exhale on a deep "Voo..." letting it vibrate through chest and belly.
- Repeat 4–6 rounds, pausing between if you get lightheaded.
- Let the sound be a drum—steady, unapologetic, yours.

Why it helps: Vibration engages vagal tone; the sound cuts through mental noise and drops you back into your body.

5. Micro-Moments You Can Hide in Plain Sight (30–45 seconds)

BYRD = Belonging + Yielding | Root = System

- Boxless Box: Breathe in, soft pause, breathe out, soft pause—no counting, just corners of calm.
- Palm Anchor: Press thumb into palm, feel pulse, take one gentle exhale longer than inhale.

- Gaze Soften: Unfocus your eyes for two breaths; let your visual field widen. Tell your body, *"No predator here."*

Building Your Breathwork Sanctuary (It's a Whole Room)

Your room is a declaration: I am sacred ground.

- Comfort: cushioned chair, yoga mat, weighted throw.

- Scent & Flame: lavender, frankincense, or whatever your lineage loves; candles you light for only you.

- Symbols: elephants for memory and majesty; photos of your daughters; an altar shelf for notes you write to future-you.

- Joy Library: books that are not for work. Pleasure is regulation.

- Sound: a tiny speaker for rain sounds, jazz, or your grandmother's favorite hymns.

Return here before crisis. Let the room remember you even when you forget yourself.

The Commitment: The Breath That Heals

(Belonging + Yielding Root—Healing in the Presence of Love)

One night, after a day that felt like it would split me open, I retreated to my healing room.
The air was low-lit and thick with lavender and candlelight. My elephants stood watch in silence, their shadows long across the wall, steady, unmoving, ancient.

I sat down on the mat, still wearing the day's armor: the polite smiles, the calm tone, the brave face I wore for everyone else. My breath was shallow and uneven, my heart galloping from battles I hadn't even named out loud. I closed my eyes, placed a hand over my chest, and began the Voo.

The sound trembled at first, soft, hesitant, then grew fuller, vibrating through my ribs like a low drumbeat from somewhere older than me. Each exhale loosened a knot I didn't know I'd tied. I could feel my body remembering itself, my nervous system whispering, *"You're home now."*

Tommy was there, not hovering, not interrupting, just sitting a few feet away in the chair near my bookshelf. The light from the candles flickered across his face. He didn't ask what was wrong. He didn't offer advice. He just breathed with me, steady and slow, until our rhythms synced like two heartbeats in conversation.

When I finally exhaled the last long Voo, the room was silent except for the sound of my own trembling breath settling into stillness.
Tommy looked at me, not with pity, but with knowing, and said softly,

"You don't have to carry all of this alone."

Something broke open in me then—not in pain, but in relief.
I didn't realize how long I had been holding my breath for everyone else—my patients, my students, my family. I had forgotten what it felt like to be held. Not as a clinician. Not as a mother. Not as a survivor. But as a woman, tired, sacred, and still worthy of care.

Presence is medicine.
Being held is medicine.
Breath makes room for both.

In that moment, I understood what *Yielding* really means in the BYRD Model; it is the holy art of letting go into support, of allowing rest to rise where striving used to live.
My body, once a battlefield, became an altar again.

As the candlelight danced against the walls, I placed my hand on my heart and whispered a small prayer:

"Thank you, breath. Thank you, body. Thank you, love."

It was not a grand healing. It was a quiet one, slow, subtle, cellular.

But that night, the rhythm of my breathing and the steady presence of my husband became one truth made flesh:

healing is not solitary work. It is communal. It is embodied.

And sometimes, the most sacred thing we can do is to let someone sit beside us while we learn how to breathe again.

Red Flags of Compassion Fatigue
(Your Body's Early Alerts)

Belonging (Body) Alerts

- Shallow breathing, sighing, jaw clenching, headaches by noon.

Yielding Alerts

- Numbness in session, dreading certain clients, irritability at small asks.

Resilience Alerts

- "I'll rest later" is your daily mantra; joy tasks feel like chores.

Disruption Alerts

- You stop naming harm; you apologize for taking breaks; you say "yes" while your body screams "no."

If two or more show up for 3+ days: scale back, switch to micro-breath, protect sleep, ask for witness (trusted friend, elder, minister).

The BYRD Model:
Breathwork Map for Compassion Fatigue

B—Belonging (Body Root): *Claim your breath.*

- Morning hand-to-heart/belly; three soft sighs; whisper your name like a blessing.

Y—Yielding (Somatic Root): *Let the body lead.*

- Between-session long exhales; doorway resets; drop the shoulders on purpose.

R—Resilience (Story Root): *Rewrite the narrative.*

- On inhale: *"I am safe."* On exhale: *"I release."*

- Journal one line: "Today my breath chose me when ______."

D—Disruption (System Root): *Make boundaries audible.*

- Out loud (even alone): *"I'm taking two minutes to breathe now."*

- Decline one nonessential ask per day. Your exhale is your no.

7-Day "Breath Sabbatical" (Realistic + Repeatable)

- Day 1 (Arrange): Set up your room; choose your candle, chair, playlist. 5 minutes.

- Day 2 (Arrive): Morning hand-to-heart/belly (2 minutes).

- Day 3 (Release): Add between-session exhale resets (3 times).

- Day 4 (Resound): Practice Voo (3 minutes) before bed.

- Day 5 (Re-story): Inhale *"I belong,"* exhale *"I am allowed"* (2 minutes).

- Day 6 (Relate): Breathe with someone you trust—two shared minutes, no words.

- Day 7 (Reflect): Journal: *What did my breath teach me about my limits and my needs?* Choose one boundary to keep.

Sacred Closing: Breath as Reclamation

Compassion fatigue taught me that breath is not extra; it's essential. It is how we refuse smallness. How we refuse to disappear inside the work. How Black bodies, and all our BIPOC kin, reclaim regulation in a world that profits from our depletion.

Breathe like you belong.
Yield like your body knows the way.
Rise with every exhale.
Disrupt the lie that you must earn your rest.

In the stillness of your room, with elephants keeping watch and your joy library close, may your breath keep writing the story your nervous system longs to live: *I am here. I am whole. I am held.*

Part IV:
Healing In
Practice

Chapter 32
Somatic Experiencing: Releasing Trauma and Building Resilience

(Body + Sacred Root—Coming Home to the Body)

Opening Reflection: The Body Remembers

Trauma does not vanish with time; it waits.

It lingers in the breath, curls inside the muscles, hums beneath the skin.

It is not just a story to be told; it is a vibration, a pattern, a pulse.

For Black clinicians, trauma lives on two frequencies: the personal and the collective.

It is the inherited tremor of ancestral survival and the daily static of navigating systems that were never built with our safety in mind. Each microaggression, each coded dismissal, each "Are you sure you belong here?" compounds into a nervous system that stays braced, even in rest.

Somatic Experiencing (SE) gives us permission to listen to the language of the body, a language older than words and wiser than intellect.

It teaches us that trauma is not the story of what happened; it's the residue of what our bodies could not finish. It is incomplete survival energy waiting to be metabolized.

For Black bodies, constantly conditioned to endure, SE becomes both healing and protest, a reclamation of what was always sacred: the right to feel, the right to rest, the right to release.

Core Principles of Somatic Experiencing and Racialized Trauma

(System + Somatic Roots—Reclaiming Regulation in an Unregulated World)

Trauma, in its essence, is not the event itself; it's what happens inside us when we are left without completion, connection, or choice.
For many Black and Brown clinicians, this "incompletion" is not occasional; it's chronic. Systems demand we stay composed while erasing our distress. Institutions praise our professionalism while punishing our pain.

Somatic Experiencing invites the body to finish what it started, to find the exits that oppression has long kept closed.

1. Pendulation—The Art of Moving Between Stress and Safety

Pendulation is the dance between contraction and release, tension and ease. It is how the body reminds itself that it can return to safety, that survival is not the only song it knows.

When trauma is racialized, pendulation becomes harder. Our nervous systems often stay suspended in readiness: a jaw slightly clenched, a diaphragm barely expanding, a smile held just long enough to survive another meeting.

How to Practice:

1. Notice where stress lives in your body, perhaps the tightness in your throat, the ache in your lower back, or the buzz beneath your skin.

2. Stay there, just for a moment, observing. No fixing. No fleeing.

3. Now, shift attention to a place of neutrality or comfort, the texture of your clothing, the steadiness of your seat, the warmth in your palms.

4. Move between both sensations: stress and ease, contraction and release.

Why It Works:

Each time we oscillate between discomfort and calm, we teach our bodies that tension is temporary. The nervous system begins to trust that it can experience intensity without drowning in it. Pendulation restores flexibility, a nervous system that bends instead of breaks.

2. Titration—Healing in Microdoses

(Yielding Root—Slowing the Rush to Recover)

Titration is SE's reminder that healing does not happen in one heroic moment; it happens in small, sacred increments.
As Black healers, and healers of color, we are often asked to "move on," to "stay strong," to "not make it about race." But true repair requires slowness. It requires reverence for what the body can hold at any given time.

How to Practice:

1. Choose one small fragment of a memory or emotion, not the whole story, just a thread.

2. Let your body notice it: where does it live? How big is it?

3. If the wave rises too high, pause. Shift attention to grounding

sensations, your breath, the press of your feet into the floor, the sound of your surroundings.

4. Return only when ready. Healing happens in chapters, not all at once.

Why It Works:
Titration prevents overwhelm and re-traumatization. It builds tolerance slowly, honoring the nervous system's pacing rather than society's pressure to "get over it."

3. Completion of Defensive Responses—Releasing Stuck Survival Energy

(Resilience Root—Finishing What the Body Began)

The body remembers every "no" it wasn't allowed to speak.
Every clench it couldn't complete.
Every time it had to stay still to stay safe.

Completion gives those silenced impulses a voice. It allows us to finish the movement, literal or symbolic, that our bodies began in the moment of threat but could not complete.

How to Practice:

1. Recall a moment when your body wanted to act, to shout, to run, to protect, but couldn't.

2. Where do you feel that energy now?

3. Allow your body a micro-expression of that impulse: a push of the palms, a roll of the shoulders, a full exhale.

4. If trembling, sighing, or spontaneous movement arises, let it. This is your nervous system completing the story.

Why It Works:
What cannot be expressed becomes compressed. Completion unravels the frozen energy that fuels chronic stress, allowing life force to flow again.

Somatic Experiencing Practices for Daily Regulation

(Belonging + Story Roots—Creating Everyday Rituals of Release)

1. Grounding After High-Stress Sessions

- Sit or stand with both feet pressing into the earth.

- Apply gentle pressure to your thighs; feel your weight supported.

- Take a slow inhale and an even slower sigh.

- Name out loud: one thing you see, one thing you hear, one thing you feel.

Why It Works:
Naming sensory details reorients the brain to the present, reminding the body that it has survived the moment.

2. Shaking Practice—The Body's Natural Reset

Animals tremble after escaping danger; humans suppress it.
To shake is to reclaim instinct.

- Stand with feet hip-width apart.

- Start by shaking your hands, then arms, then legs.

- Let the movement grow without performance or precision.

- After one or two minutes, pause. Notice what shifts, warmth, tingling, release.

Why It Works:
Shaking releases cortisol, rebalances the vagal system, and signals to the body: the danger has passed.

3. The Voo Breath—Vibrating the Sacred Back into the System

The Voo is sound medicine.

- Inhale through the nose.
- Exhale with a deep, resonant "Vooooo..."—let it vibrate in your chest like a sermon note from your ancestors.
- Repeat 3–5 rounds.

Why It Works:
This vibration stimulates the vagus nerve, restoring regulation through resonance. It's a nervous system hymn—part science, part spirit.

A Personal Reflection: From Collapse to Completion

After my stroke, I lived in the gap between collapse and survival, my body remembering danger even in silence. During recovery, SE became a sacred map back to wholeness.

One morning, as I practiced gentle pendulation, I felt a subtle shake in my right hand. It startled me. Then came tears, not from pain but release. My body was remembering its own unfinished movement, the moment of freezing at my desk when everything went numb. That trembling was not weakness; it was wisdom. It was my nervous system writing the ending I never got to live.

Somatic Experiencing taught me this truth:
Healing is not about forcing calm, it's about restoring choice.
And choice is the foundation of freedom.

Closing Reflection:
Reclaiming the Body as a Safer Place

(Sacred Root—Liberation Through Embodiment)

For Black clinicians, the body is not just a vessel, it is a record. It carries the songs, the scars, and the strength of generations who survived the unspeakable.

Somatic Experiencing invites us to rewrite that record, not by erasing pain, but by reuniting with our capacity for aliveness.

Healing does not mean forgetting. It means movement. It means returning to rhythm. It means allowing the nervous system to know:
"The threat has passed. I am here. I am whole."

As you integrate these practices, remember: you are not just restoring your own regulation, you are modeling liberation for those who come after you.

Each tremor, each exhale, each gentle pause becomes an ancestral prayer in motion.

Your body is not your enemy.
It is your inheritance.
It is your sanctuary.
It is your revolution.

CHAPTER 33
THE ROLE OF SOMATIC EXPERIENCING IN MY HEALING

(Body + Belonging Root—Learning to Trust My Body Again)

Learning to Trust My Body Again

After my stroke, my body felt like an unfamiliar place, a landscape altered by trauma, no longer predictable, no longer safe. My nervous system was frayed, my breath erratic, my muscles holding a tension I could not name. I had spent years pushing through, overriding discomfort, ignoring fatigue, and minimizing pain, the way so many Black women are conditioned to. But my body had reached its limit. It was no longer asking me to slow down. It was demanding it.

Somatic Experiencing (SE) became a bridge back to myself. It was not a quick fix, nor was it a neat and orderly process. Healing was messy—some days, my body responded with ease; other days it resisted, stiff and unyielding. But SE gave me a language to communicate with my nervous system, to understand its signals rather than fear them.

I learned that my body was not broken; it was protecting me in the only way it knew how. And if I could meet it with patience rather than frustration, I could begin to rebuild my relationship with it.

SE as a Daily Practice

During my recovery, I incorporated SE into my daily life in ways both intentional and intuitive. It was not about setting aside an hour for structured therapy, it was about finding moments of regulation in the small, everyday interactions that anchored me in safety.

Pendulation: Moving Between Fear and Safety

Instead of forcing myself to push past fear, I learned to move gently between discomfort and safety, allowing my nervous system to pendulate naturally.

How I Practiced:
When waves of fear or anxiety surfaced, I allowed myself to feel them fully, not suppressing, not avoiding, but simply acknowledging their presence.
Then, I brought my awareness to something that signaled safety, the warmth of Tommy's hand on mine, the sound of my daughters laughing in the next room, or even the sensation of the ground beneath my feet.
I moved back and forth between these states—from distress to ease, from fear to grounding, reminding my nervous system that it could return to safety at any time.

Why It Worked:
Pendulation disrupted the cycle of fear, preventing me from becoming stuck in hypervigilance or shutdown. It showed my body that safety was not an abstraction but a real, felt experience I could return to at will.

Titration: Facing Trauma in Small, Manageable Pieces

The enormity of my trauma felt overwhelming, too big, too vast to face all at once. My nervous system shut down at the thought of processing it all, so instead, I focused on small pieces.

How I Practiced:
I did not force myself to revisit the entire experience of my stroke or the racialized stress leading up to it. Instead, I focused on a single sensation, a

single emotion, a single fragment of the memory at a time.

If distress built too quickly, I shifted to something grounding, running my fingers along a soft blanket, pressing my feet into the floor, or focusing on the steady inhale and exhale of my breath.

I reminded myself: I do not have to heal all at once. Small moments of release are just as powerful as big breakthroughs.

Why It Worked:

Titration allowed my body to process trauma without becoming overwhelmed. It built resilience by showing me that I could face difficult emotions in small doses, and still be okay.

Orienting: Reclaiming My Sense of Safety in the Present

After my stroke, certain environments felt unsafe, even when they posed no actual threat. My body remained on high alert, as if bracing for the next crisis. Orienting helped me signal to my nervous system that I was not in danger.

How I Practiced:

I took slow, deliberate moments to look around my space, identifying things that signaled safety, the color of the walls, the sound of music playing, the way the sunlight filtered through the window.

When I felt anxiety creeping in, I asked myself:

Where am I right now?

What do I see, hear, and feel that tells me I am safe?

This anchored me in the present, reminding my body that I was not in the past, not in the hospital, not in crisis anymore.

Why It Worked:

Orienting prevented me from being trapped in trauma loops. It helped my nervous system register the reality of safety, rather than the perception of threat.

The Commitment: The Dance Between Release and Rest

SE taught me that healing is not linear, it is a dance between release and rest, between grief and gratitude. Some days, my body let go with ease, through shaking, deep sighs, or gentle movement. Other days, it held on, unwilling to soften.

I learned to respect both.

Healing is not about forcing progress, it is about meeting the body where it is and trusting that it will guide the process at its own pace.
SE reminded me that my body was never the enemy, it was the site of my survival. It carried me through trauma not to betray me, but to protect me. And in that realization, I found something unexpected: gratitude.

Closing Reflection:
Honoring the Body's Wisdom

For so long, I treated my body as something to manage, control, or push past. SE taught me that healing begins with listening.

My body was not failing me, it was communicating with me.
My nervous system was not broken, it was doing its best to keep me safe.
I did not have to force healing—it would come, in time, as I made
space for it.

Now, when I practice SE, I do so not as a chore, but as an act of self-respect. It is how I remind myself:
I am safe in my body.
I am allowed to rest.
I do not have to hold everything alone.

May we all learn to listen to the wisdom within us, and trust that healing, no matter how slow, is always unfolding.

Chapter 34
Exercises Tailored for Black & POC Clinicians in High-Stress Environments

(Resilience + System Roots—Healing in the Midst of Harm)

For Black clinicians, the work of healing extends beyond the therapy room. We are not just holding space for our clients; we are navigating the weight of systemic oppression, workplace microaggressions, and the emotional labor that comes with being "the only one" in predominantly white spaces. This constant state of vigilance takes a toll, not just emotionally but physiologically.

Somatic Experiencing offers tangible, body-centered tools to discharge stress, reclaim agency, and restore balance. The following exercises are tailored for Black clinicians who navigate high-stress environments daily. These practices are not about bypassing or ignoring systemic harm—they are about cultivating nervous system resilience so that stress does not become embedded in the body.

1. Reclaiming Agency Through Micro-Movements

Systemic challenges can leave you feeling powerless, as if every part of you is weighed down by the demands and injustices of the world. Micro-movements serve as a reminder that even in the smallest acts, we have agency.

Often, racial trauma locks the body into patterns of tension, bracing, or constriction, reinforcing a sense of stuckness. Small, intentional movements can reawaken the nervous system's ability to shift out of these patterns, restoring a sense of control.

Exercise: Clench and Release

- Sit in a quiet space and bring your awareness to your hands.

- Slowly clench your fists, feeling the tension build.

- Hold for a few moments, acknowledging the sensation.

- Gently release, noticing the shift as your fingers unfurl.

- Repeat several times, paying attention to how your body responds.

Personal Reflection:
This exercise has been a lifeline for me. After particularly heavy days, when microaggressions, workplace stress, or the exhaustion of proving my competence threatened to overwhelm me, I would sit at my desk or in my car, clenching and releasing my hands.
Each squeeze was a silent acknowledgment of the tension I carried. Each release was a reminder that I did not have to hold onto it.

Why It Works:

- Signals to the nervous system that release is possible, even when the mind feels trapped.

- Helps discharge excess stress energy rather than storing it in the muscles.

- Reinforces a sense of agency, reminding you that you are not powerless in the face of stress.

2. Ancestral Connection for Strength

Our ancestors are more than just memories. They are our roots, our foundation, a lineage of resilience and survival. When the weight of the world feels unbearable, connecting with them can be profoundly grounding.

Racialized trauma often creates a sense of isolation, a feeling of being unprotected in hostile environments. But we are never alone. We carry the wisdom, the courage, and the strength of those who came before us.

When Tommy and I traveled to Africa, something ancient stirred within us. The moment my feet touched the red soil, I felt a current move through me, steady, electric, alive. The air was different, the rhythm slower, sacred. It wasn't just a trip; it was a return. A remembering.

I could feel the pulse of generations humming beneath my soles, a vibration that whispered, *"Welcome home."* Tommy and I didn't need words. We just stood there, hands intertwined, hearts open, as tears welled up, uninvited but holy. For the first time in a long time, my body exhaled without hesitation.

The land held us like an embrace from the ancestors themselves. The trees, the wind, the distant sound of drumming—all of it conspired to remind me that I am part of something vast and enduring. I understood then that healing isn't always about mending; sometimes it's about remembering who you were before the wound.

Returning to the Motherland was not just a journey across oceans; it was a journey back to belonging.

Exercise: Calling in the Ancestors

- Find a quiet, comfortable space where you feel safe.
- Close your eyes and imagine your ancestors standing behind you.
- Picture their faces, their hands resting gently on your shoulders.
- Visualize them whispering words of encouragement and love.
- Feel their presence as a shield of strength and resilience.

Personal Reflection:

After my stroke, I leaned heavily on this practice. There were nights in rehab when fear crept in, especially as I struggled with sleep apnea. The mask I wore to help me breathe felt suffocating, amplifying my sense of vulnerability. Some nights, I couldn't keep it on, the weight of it triggering a panic that felt beyond my control.

But as I lay there, I would visualize my ancestors standing beside me, strong, steady, and present. I imagined their voices:
"You are not alone. You come from strength. You are worthy of healing."

Slowly, my breath steadied. My body softened. The fear loosened its grip.

Why It Works:

- Activates co-regulation, allowing the nervous system to feel held and supported.

- Counters racial trauma's message of isolation by reinforcing connection to a larger lineage.

- Shifts focus from fear to resilience, reminding us that we have inherited survival wisdom.

3. Discharging Workday Tension

The body accumulates stress like a sponge. Each tense conversation, each microaggression swallowed, each moment of holding back when we should have been able to exhale freely, it all builds up. If not intentionally released, this stress lodges itself in the muscles, the breath, and the nervous system, turning into chronic tension, insomnia, and emotional exhaustion.

This exercise provides a gentle way to reset, allowing the body to offload the day's burdens rather than carry them into tomorrow.

Exercise: Breath and Body Scan for Release

- Lie down in a comfortable position, perhaps with a soft blanket or weighted pillow.

- Close your eyes and let your breath flow naturally, neither forcing nor controlling it.

- Gently scan your body, noticing where tension resides—tight shoulders, clenched jaw, tension in the lower back.

- With each exhale, imagine the tension dissolving, as if your breath is carrying it away.

Personal Reflection:

I often practiced this exercise late at night, once my house was finally quiet. Some nights, Tommy would lie next to me, his rhythmic breaths syncing with mine.

In those moments, the simple act of breathing together became an anchor, a reminder that healing does not have to be solitary.

Why It Works:

- Helps down-regulate the nervous system after prolonged stress.

- Reinforces the connection between breath and release.

- Prepares the body for deeper rest and nervous system repair.

The Commitment: Embodying the Right to Release

For Black clinicians, the expectation of endurance is relentless. We are often the ones expected to hold it all together, to be the strong one, the advocate, the mentor, the healer. But healing cannot happen if we are constantly bracing against harm without moments of release.

These exercises are not just about stress relief; they are about rewiring the nervous system to know that release is safe, that rest is allowed, that agency is ours to reclaim.

Micro-movements remind us we have control, even in small ways.
Ancestral connection reinforces that we are never alone in our struggles.

Breath and body scanning help us unload what we were never meant to carry indefinitely.

Healing is not about being unbreakable. It is about learning when to soften, when to rest, and when to let go.
May these practices serve as a reminder: your nervous system deserves care, your breath deserves space, and your body deserves release.

Chapter 35
Integrating SE Into My Healing Journey

(Returning to the Roots of Belonging, Yielding, Resilience, and Disruption)

The Valley: Revisiting the Stroke

My stroke was more than a medical event; it was a reckoning. A moment when my body demanded what I had long denied it: rest, acknowledgment, and healing.

For so long, I had been running—from exhaustion, from systemic stress, from the burden of always needing to be "the strong one." But my body refused to keep up the pace. It forced me to stop. To listen.

In the days following my stroke, my husband, Tommy, became my anchor. He stayed by my side in rehab, reminding me of my strength when I doubted it. One evening, as tears streamed down my face, I whispered,

"What if I can't go back to who I was?"

He gently held my hand and said,

"Maybe this is your chance to become someone even stronger."

His words settled in my body like medicine.

I had a choice—to see my stroke as the end of something or the beginning of something new.

That is when I fully leaned into Somatic Experiencing (SE). Not as an abstract concept, but as a lifeline—a daily, embodied practice of reclaiming my safety, my body, and my healing.

The Rise: SE Practices That Transformed My Healing

Integrating SE into my recovery was not about finding one "right" technique; it was about building a toolkit of strategies I could draw upon in moments of fear, fatigue, or fragility.

I needed ways to anchor myself in the present when fear overwhelmed me, release survival energy trapped in my body, and reconnect with the parts of me that still felt whole.

1. Grounding Through Soothing Rocking

After my stroke, fear came in waves—the fear of not recovering fully, of never feeling like myself again. I needed something gentle, rhythmic, and instinctive, something that reminded my body of safety without demanding effort or thought.

Exercise: Soothing Rocking Practice

- Sit comfortably in a chair with your feet flat on the floor.

- Begin to slowly rock forward and back, or side to side, just enough to feel the weight shift beneath you.

- Let your breath naturally follow the motion.

- If it feels supportive, hum softly or exhale through parted lips as you move.

- Notice the contact between your body and the chair, the ground, the air around you.
  Let the rhythm soothe you, like the ocean's tide, a steady reminder that motion can mean safety, not danger.

Why it helped:
This movement reintroduced my body to comfort through rhythm. Rocking evoked the primal memory of being held, of breath syncing with heartbeat. It gave me a way to calm my nervous system without needing to fix or perform, just to sway, to feel, to be.

2. Reclaiming Strength Through Micro-Movements

One of the hardest parts of recovery was rebuilding trust in my body. Even small movements felt uncertain. Somatic Experiencing taught me that big change begins with small movement, that power can return in quiet, measured ways.

Exercise: Finger and Foot Flexing

- Find a comfortable seat.
- Slowly curl your fingers into a loose fist, then extend them fully.
- Repeat with your toes.
- Notice the stability of what supports you—floor, chair, or lap.

Why it helped:
Each movement reminded me of agency. It wasn't about physical strength; it was about reclaiming relationship with my body, one gentle act at a time.

3. Releasing Held Trauma Through Humming Breath

Sleep apnea made rest feel dangerous. Some nights, the thought of sleep triggered panic instead of peace.
Humming helped me find safety in sound, activating the vagus nerve, soothing the fear of losing control.

Exercise: The Humming Exhale

- Inhale through your nose.
- Exhale with a low, steady hum.

- Feel the vibration resonate through your chest and throat.
- Continue until calm returns.

Why it helped:
The vibration anchored me. It softened the edges of panic and invited my body back into safety. It was my reminder: breath is both presence and prayer.

4. Completing My Nervous System's Stress Cycle

Even after the hospital released me, tension lingered. My body still held the echo of fear and fatigue. SE reminded me that unfinished survival energy must move, so I learned to shake, sway, and let it go.

Exercise: Full-Body Shaking and Release

- Stand with feet hip-width apart.
- Start by shaking your hands, then let the movement spread— arms, shoulders, hips, legs.
- Breathe.
- Let emotions move through—sighs, yawns, tears.
- When finished, pause and feel the quiet after the storm.

Why it helped:
Movement gave my body permission to complete what trauma interrupted. I wasn't just surviving anymore; I was releasing.

The Commitment: Choosing to Stay Present

Integrating SE into my healing was not about returning to who I was before; it was about trusting the version of me that emerged after.

Grounding taught me to stay steady in chaos.
Micro-movements reminded me of the quiet power of progress.

Humming taught me that my own breath could hold me.
Shaking gave me back my freedom to feel.

Healing is not linear; it is relational. It is the dialogue between my body and my spirit, between what broke and what is still becoming whole.

And through it all, Tommy's quiet presence, his steady hand, his unwavering belief, became my reminder of Belonging.
He didn't try to fix me. He just stayed. His calm nervous system met mine, and that co-regulation became its own medicine.

Building Resilience for the Future

Somatic Experiencing has taught me that healing is not about erasing pain; it's about integrating it. Every challenge, from racialized stress to illness, has shaped me, but it no longer defines me.

For Black clinicians, resilience is often demanded but rarely supported. We are taught to pour endlessly without replenishment. SE redefines resilience, not as endurance, but as restoration.

It invites us to yield instead of push, to rest instead of prove, to breathe instead of brace.
It's a reclamation of agency, a disruption of the inherited expectation to carry it all alone.

Each time I listen to my body instead of silencing it, I am healing.
Each time I honor rest instead of resisting it, I am remembering my worth.
Each time I create stillness amid chaos, I am protecting the next generation from the exhaustion I once normalized.

Closing Reflection: The BYRD Within

Trauma leaves its mark, but so does healing.
Through SE, I have learned to live in alignment with my own model:

Belonging—My body is not my enemy; it is my home.
Yielding—Rest is not weakness; it is wisdom.
Resilience—My strength is not new; it is inherited.
Disruption—I no longer measure my worth by endurance.

This journey is my declaration that healing is not passive; it is revolutionary.
And every time I breathe deeply, move gently, or let my body tremble and release, I am saying to myself and to those who will follow:

"I am here.
I am healing.
I am free."

CHAPTER 36
REST AS RESISTANCE: HEALING FROM COMPASSION FATIGUE

Opening Reflection: The Sacred Pause

For BIPOC clinicians, the act of rest is radical.
We were taught to survive, not to stop.
To serve, not to soften.
To carry, not to release.

But the body keeps score, of every client's tears we held, every microaggression we swallowed, every hour we worked past the edge of depletion. And eventually, it demands a reckoning.

This chapter is that reckoning.
It is where the four roots of the BYRD Model converge:

Belonging—through community that holds us when we fall.
Yielding—through the sacred pause that honors the body's limits.
Resilience—through the rebuilding that follows rest.
Disruption—through the refusal to martyr ourselves for systems that will never love us back.

To rest is to resist the lie that our worth is in our work.
To breathe deeply is to reclaim our humanity.
To stop shrinking is to return home to ourselves.

The Valley: When Compassion Becomes Depletion

There was a season when I mistook endurance for strength.

I pushed through fatigue, answered one more email, took one more session, held one more story heavy with grief.

By the end of each day, I was hollow.

My compassion had turned into depletion.

The week before my stroke, I remember sitting in my car after work, the steering wheel cool beneath my palms, and feeling nothing, no tears, no energy, no pulse of purpose. Just stillness and shame.

That's what compassion fatigue looks like when it's rooted in systemic harm. It's not just exhaustion; it's erasure.

And in that moment, the BYRD roots whispered softly from somewhere deep within:

"Yield. Stop pushing. Your body is asking for sanctuary."

The Rise: When Connection Becomes Medicine

When I finally called Jevita, my sister from my Somatic Experiencing cohort, I didn't need advice; I needed witnessing.

She didn't rush to fix it. She didn't give me a checklist of self-care tasks.

She simply said, softly,

"Some people are only meant to walk with you for a season. And that's okay."

That sentence landed like medicine.

Because rest is not always about sleep, it's about surrender.

It's about letting go of the people, roles, and expectations that keep us overextended.

Community became my co-regulation.
Belonging became my breath.

And in that sacred moment of stillness, I felt the roots of the BYRD
Model awaken again inside me—
steady, pulsing, alive—
reminding me that I am not alone in this work.

The Commitment: Rest as a Form of Disruption

I had spent my entire career holding space for others, believing that
if I just gave a little more, I could somehow fix what was broken in
the system.
But the truth was, the system was feeding on my exhaustion.

So I began to disrupt, not with rage, but with rest.
I began saying no to overextension.
I began taking days off without apology.
I began honoring the Yielding Root, the part of me that knows sacred rest
is not laziness; it's liberation.

When I rest, I refuse to participate in a system that profits from my
depletion.
When I rest, I model Resilience for those who come after me.
When I rest, I Disrupt the myth that my worth is tied to how much I
can endure.

Rest became the revolution my nervous system had been waiting for.

The Lesson: Healing Requires Boundaries

There is nothing noble about martyrdom.
We are not meant to hold it all.
We are not meant to prove our strength through suffering.

It was my therapist, Valerie, who first taught me this truth.
In one of our sessions, she said gently,

"Sis, boundaries aren't barriers, Sharlisa, they're bridges back to yourself."

That line stayed with me. It was the invitation I didn't know I needed—the permission to stop performing resilience and start embodying it.

Each time I press my palms together and breathe, I hear her words again and remind myself:

"I do not have to carry everything.
I do not have to carry everyone.
My rest is my revolution."

Boundaries are not walls, they are roots.
They ground us.
They nourish us.
They help us grow again after seasons of depletion.

Closing Reflection: Returning to the Body

In *The Deepest Well*, Dr. Nadine Burke Harris writes,

"Healing doesn't mean erasing the past, it means giving ourselves what we needed back then but never received."

That's what rest has become for me, an act of re-parenting, of offering my body the care it begged for long before the stroke, long before the collapse.

Every pause is a promise.
Every breath is a boundary.
Every act of rest is a reclamation.

So to my fellow healers, especially those whose skin carries the story of endurance—

May you learn that rest is not retreat; it's revival.
May you find the courage to Yield before you break.
May you remember that your body is not a battlefield; it's a garden.

Tend to it.
Breathe in it.
Belong to it.

Chapter 37
Self-Care Practices Tailored to Black and POC Clinicians

Opening Reflection: Self-Care as Sacred Reclamation

For BIPOC clinicians, self-care is not indulgence; it is *survival.* We navigate the silent weight of systemic oppression, microaggressions, and emotional labor every day. Every session we hold, every institution we navigate, every moment we must code-switch or prove our competence in systems not built for us, takes something from our bodies.

Healing, then, must be intentional, radical, and deeply personal.
It is not about scented candles or spa days; it is about *sovereignty.*
It is the process of remembering that our rest, our boundaries, and our breath belong to us.

Each act of self-care becomes an invocation of the BYRD roots:

- Belonging—reclaiming connection in a world that isolates.

- Yielding—surrendering to stillness without shame.

- Resilience—rising again, not through grind, but through grace.

- Disruption—defying systems that equate our worth with exhaustion.

1. Building Boundaries as a Form of Resistance

For BIPOC clinicians, boundary-setting is not self-protection; it's *rebellion.*

In systems that demand more, boundaries are how we say, *"I will not be consumed."*

Strategies for Setting Boundaries

- Resist excessive workload demands. Just because you can take on more does not mean you should.

- Say "no" with intention—a full sentence. No explanation required.

- Define and protect work hours—Guard them as you would sacred prayer.

Personal Reflection

As both a professor and a clinician, I used to say yes to everything: extra clients, committees, lectures, trainings. I thought saying yes was how you proved worthiness. But each yes carved away at my peace.

The first time I said no, it felt like rebellion, and then, relief.
No was not rejection. It was return.
It was Yielding in practice: slowing down to honor what my nervous system already knew: *you cannot pour from a vessel that keeps cracking.*

Why It Works

- Prevents burnout and compassion fatigue.

- Reinforces self-worth beyond productivity.

- Creates sacred time for restoration.

2. Daily Grounding Practices

For BIPOC clinicians, grounding is not optional; it's *oxygen*.
We hold so much: the grief of clients, the rage of injustice, the ache of invisibility. Our bodies need anchors to remind us that we still exist beyond the pain.

Grounding Practices

- Morning meditation or prayer.

- Somatic movement, gentle rocking, stretching, or mindful shaking.

- Slow, rhythmic breathing to re-activate safety.

Personal Reflection
Some mornings, I step outside barefoot before sunrise. The air is cool; the world still half asleep. I place my palm on the nearest tree and whisper a prayer of thanks. Its bark against my skin reminds me: *You are rooted. You are alive. You are of the earth.*

Sometimes Tommy joins me.
He doesn't say much; he just stands beside me, coffee in hand, letting silence do the work. His quiet presence grounds me; his steadiness tells my nervous system, *you are safe now.*

On the hardest days, when my mind is racing and my breath shallow, he'll place a hand at the base of my neck and say softly,

"Breathe, baby. The world can wait a minute."

And in that minute, I return to myself.

Why It Works

- Interrupts chronic stress patterns.

- Encourages somatic release.

- Creates rituals of safety and belonging.

3. Prioritizing Rest and Recovery

For BIPOC clinicians, rest is not a luxury; it is a *revolution*.
In systems that equate worth with output, our rest becomes a protest, a refusal to be machinery.

Tips for Rest

- Schedule rest as nonnegotiable.
- Develop bedtime rituals that cue safety: dimmed lights, quiet music, gratitude journaling.
- Listen to the body's whisper before it screams.

Personal Reflection
After my stroke, rest became sacred. My body had been begging for stillness long before it collapsed. Now, when fatigue creeps in, Tommy notices before I do.

He'll gently close my laptop or take my phone and say, "You've done enough for today."
At first, I resisted; it felt strange to be cared for without earning it. But over time, I realized: his protection wasn't about control; it was about *love witnessing exhaustion.*

He would sit beside me while I rested, reading his Bible or humming softly, his presence like a weighted blanket.
Rest stopped feeling like surrender. It became communion.

As Tricia Hersey writes in *Rest Is Resistance,*

"Rest is a portal to healing."

For me, it is also a doorway to intimacy, to being held, seen, and allowed to be fully human.

Why It Works

- Reduces systemic and physical stress.

- Rebuilds resilience through parasympathetic activation.

- Reclaims the right to be unproductive and still worthy.

4. Connecting with Community

Healing in isolation is a myth.
We are communal beings; our nervous systems are wired for connection.
For BIPOC clinicians, belonging is medicine.

Ways to Build Community

- Join BIPOC professional networks or healing collectives.

- Find peer support or supervision spaces that honor identity.

- Nurture friendships that remind you who you are beyond your role.

Personal Reflection
When I felt invisible in institutional spaces, Jevita became my mirror.
She reminded me, "You don't have to heal alone."
And when I forgot that truth, Tommy echoed it in his own quiet way,
showing up with dinner, insisting I step away from my laptop, holding
me in prayer when my spirit was weary.

Between them, I found Belonging again, community in both sisterhood
and love, proof that co-regulation can come in many forms.

Why It Works

- Reduces isolation in oppressive systems.

- Reinforces collective resilience.

- Normalizes the shared human need for care.

5. Creative Expression as Self-Care

Art, writing, dance, and song are ancestral medicine, ways to move grief and reclaim joy when words fail.

Creative Practices

- Journaling to release emotion or connect with ancestors.
- Singing, painting, or movement as embodied storytelling.
- Letter-writing as dialogue with your lineage.

Personal Reflection
Some evenings, Tommy turns on old jazz records and we dance in the kitchen, slow, no choreography, just rhythm and laughter.
He'll say, "You look happiest when you stop thinking."

And he's right.
That's what creativity is for me now: a return to the body's joy, unmediated, unmeasured. Watching my granddaughters paint or sing reminds me that freedom still lives in play.

Why It Works

- Releases stored emotion.
- Restores the connection between expression and healing.
- Reclaims joy as resistance.

Closing Reflection: The BYRD Roots of Self-Care

Self-care is not a checklist; it's a reclamation of power.
Each act—resting, breathing, saying no, reaching out—is a way of returning to our roots:

- Belonging—through community that sees us.
- Yielding—through rest that restores us.

- Resilience—through practices that strengthen us.
- Disruption—through boundaries that protect us.

Tommy once said, as he watched me light a candle before bed,

"You don't have to keep the fire burning all night. Let it rest. Let it glow enough for tomorrow."

That line became my mantra.
Because healing isn't about keeping the light on all the time, it's about trusting that even in darkness, the flame still lives within you.

As Tricia Hersey reminds us,

"Your healing is not a privilege, it is your birthright."

So may you rest.
May you breathe.
May you remember that tending to yourself is not stepping away from your purpose—
it *is* your purpose.
And that is enough.

Tommy's Presence as Somatic Anchor

Healing is not always solitary; it can be witnessed, held, and steadied through love.
For me, that anchor has been Tommy.

After my stroke, when my body was relearning what safety felt like, his presence became my nervous system's mirror. He never pushed. He didn't rush me toward strength. He simply stayed, quiet, patient, steady, as I found my way back to myself.

There were nights when my breath would quicken in the dark, fear curling through my body like smoke. The hum of the sleep apnea machine

felt suffocating, the room too still.
And then, his voice, low, grounded, would cut through the panic:

"I'm right here. Just breathe with me."

We would lie there, our breaths syncing like tide and shore.
In those moments, I wasn't a therapist, or a professor, or a healer trying to make sense of her own recovery. I was simply a woman learning that safety could sound like someone's steady exhale beside her.

Sometimes he'd trace slow circles on my back as I drifted into sleep, a wordless rhythm that told my body, *you are not in danger anymore.*

That is what co-regulation looks like in practice: one nervous system lending calm to another until both find equilibrium.

And that, too, is The BYRD Model

- Belonging, through presence that says *you are safe with me.*

- Yielding, in allowing myself to be cared for.

- Resilience, in learning to rest without guilt.

- Disruption, in rejecting the myth that strength means solitude.

Tommy's presence taught me that healing does not always come in therapy rooms or on meditation mats. Sometimes it arrives quietly, in the way someone listens without fixing, in the warmth of a hand placed gently over yours, in the courage it takes to let love stay when you've been taught to carry it all alone.

Love, I've learned, is not just emotional; it's *somatic.*
It lives in the nervous system.
It breathes safety back into the body.
And it reminds us that being held is also a form of healing.

CHAPTER 38
THE POWER OF BEING HELD

*C*ommunity is the heart of healing.

It is the space where we are seen, heard, and held, a sanctuary that offers restoration when the world demands more than we have to give.

For Black clinicians like me, navigating systemic injustice while carrying the emotional weight of others can feel isolating, exhausting, and, at times, impossible. The work we do is sacred, but it is also heavy. And in those moments when the burden threatens to consume us, the presence of supportive networks—spiritual, familial, professional—becomes a lifeline.

I have felt this truth in my bones.

One of my greatest sources of strength and renewal has been my spiritual community at Emmanuel Baptist Church in San Jose. Among my prayer warriors, my Monday night prayer group, Minister Katrina Barnes, and Brother Chester Hutchinson, I have found the kind of encouragement that sustains me in ways beyond words. Their unwavering belief in my purpose, their prayers when I felt too weak to pray for myself, their presence when I needed reminders of my own resilience—these moments have been anchors in my healing.

Just as my uncle Alton has been a model of professionalism and resilience in my life, my church family has shown me the power of collective care, of healing that does not happen alone but in communion with others.

This chapter is about that communion. It is about the importance of building, nurturing, and maintaining networks of care that sustain us. It is about rejecting the idea that we must struggle in isolation and instead embracing the truth that we are strongest when we heal together.

The Danger of Isolation

No one heals alone.

Yet, the weight of being a Black clinician in predominantly white spaces, the expectations of constant emotional labor, and the generational messages of endurance over ease can make it feel as though we have to bear it all alone.

Many of us have internalized the belief that:

- We should be able to "handle it" on our own.
- Asking for help is weakness.
- Seeking support is a burden to others.
- If we don't hold everything together, no one else will.

This belief system keeps us in cycles of exhaustion, resentment, and emotional depletion. I have lived this. I have spent years carrying more than I should, convincing myself that I could manage the weight.

Until my body forced me to listen.
Until burnout crept in.
Until I sat in my car after a long day of work, too exhausted to move, too empty to cry, realizing that I had spent so much time holding space for others that I had none left for myself.

That was my turning point.

Because the truth is, isolation is not a badge of honor; it is a slow erosion of self.

The Rise: The Power of Safe Community

Healing happens in relationship.

When I look at the spaces where I have felt most held, most nurtured, most restored, they are all spaces of community.

- In my church family, I have found spiritual restoration.
- In my friendships, I have found truth-tellers who remind me of my worth.
- In my Somatic Experiencing (SE) community, I have found a language for healing that speaks to my body and spirit.

Safe care is about deliberately cultivating relationships that affirm, replenish, and sustain you. It is about recognizing that we were never meant to do this alone.

In the wisdom of the Igbo people of southeastern Nigeria, there
is a saying:
"Ọ bụ mmadụ ka mmadụ ji bụrụ mmadụ."
It is through others that one becomes human.

That truth lives in my bones.
It lives in the way my sisters check in on me, the way Tommy's quiet presence steadies me after long days, and the way my daughters' laughter resets my nervous system better than any meditation app ever could.

When I traveled to Kenya and Egypt, something ancient stirred in me.
It wasn't just a trip, it was a homecoming of the soul.

In Kenya, the air carried a kind of knowing. The earth beneath my feet felt alive, familiar, as if it remembered me before I remembered myself. The rhythm of the land felt like breath made visible. I could feel the heartbeat of the ancestors moving through the wind, humming softly, "Welcome back."

And then, in Egypt, standing before the Nile and the sacred stillness of

Kemet's ancient ruins, I felt time collapse into stillness. The wind carried whispers of beginnings, the birthplace of civilization, the ground where Black brilliance and divinity were first named.

Tommy stood beside me, quiet and reverent, our hands intertwined.
Neither of us spoke. We didn't need to.
Because the silence itself was prayer.

Stepping onto that soil, I realized that belonging is not always about geography, it's about recognition.
It's the body remembering its source.
It's the spirit exhaling, saying, "Ah... home."

In that moment, I understood what the Yorùbá call Aṣẹ, the sacred life force that animates all things.
I felt it move through the land, through Tommy's hand, through my own chest as I breathed.
It was as if my ancestors gathered in the desert wind, whispering,
"You are the dream we carried. Walk freely, daughter. You belong."

That journey became one of the deepest healings of my life, not because I found something new, but because I remembered something eternal.

The Commitment: Building Supportive Networks

How do we cultivate and maintain these life-giving relationships?
Here are the foundational roots of building supportive networks that create true safe care—through the BYRD Model lens.

Belonging—Identify the People Who Truly See You

Not every relationship is nourishing, and part of belonging is discerning who truly supports you and who drains you.
Who sees you when you're not performing?
Who holds your truth without judgment?
Who celebrates your boundaries as much as your accomplishments?

There was a time when I grieved the loss of certain friendships, people I thought would always be my support system but who disappeared when I needed them most.

That grief made room for the sacred ones, the people who remind me that my softness is not a weakness but a reflection of my strength.

Yielding—Allow Yourself to Be Held

Yielding asks us to soften, to receive care instead of resisting it.
For years, I was the strong one, the helper, the one others leaned on.
Now, I practice leaning back.
I let others hold me.
I let love catch me when I fall.

This is the medicine of my church family, of Tommy's patience, of friendships that do not demand explanation.
Yielding teaches us that surrender is not collapse, it is communion.

Resilience—Nurture Reciprocal Relationships

A strong support system thrives on reciprocity, a balance of giving and receiving.
In my SE community, I learned that co-regulation is resilience in motion.
We steady each other's nervous systems when we breathe, listen, and stay present.
Resilience is not built-in isolation—it is sustained in connection.

Disruption—Find or Create Spaces That Honor You

To disrupt is to refuse assimilation.
To find or create spaces that honor your full humanity.
I have been in rooms where I had to translate my pain, where my expertise was doubted, and my authenticity muted.
Never again.

Now, I choose spaces where my laughter is medicine, my heritage is

honored, and my rest is not questioned.
If those spaces don't exist, I build them.
Because that, too, is disruption, creating a table where your wholeness is welcome.

Closing Reflection: We Heal in Community

In the Yorùbá tradition, there is a proverb:
"Eniyan l'aṣo mi."
People are my covering.

That truth is the heartbeat of this chapter.

We were never meant to heal alone.
Our liberation lives in relationship.
Our healing lives in the breath between souls, in the hands that reach out, in the quiet spaces where someone says, "You don't have to carry this by yourself."

So ask yourself:
Where am I still holding too much alone?
Who reminds me that I am safe to rest?
What communities can I nurture that will carry me forward?

Because we heal in the collective.
We rise in belonging.
And when we allow ourselves to be held, by faith, by community, by lineage—we remember what our ancestors have been whispering all along:

You are not alone.
You never were.
And the village has been waiting for you to come home.

Roots Reflection (BYRD Model Integration)

Belonging—Healing deepens when we are witnessed by those who see us fully.

Yielding—Resting in the arms of community is a sacred act of trust.

Resilience—Connection becomes the rhythm that steadies our nervous system.

Disruption—Choosing to heal together in a world that isolates us is a revolutionary act.

We do not heal in solitude.
We heal in circles, in songs, in silence shared between kindred hearts.
And when we allow ourselves to be held, we become the medicine we once sought.

(Root: Resilience)

Compassion fatigue does not appear overnight. It accumulates quietly and steadily until the body forces us to pay attention. Identifying early warning signs allows for course correction before full depletion occurs.

Consider:
Physical symptoms: persistent fatigue, tension headaches, digestive issues, or insomnia.
Emotional cues: irritability, detachment, anxiety, or resentment.
Cognitive shifts: difficulty concentrating, making decisions, or feeling present with clients and loved ones.

Personal Reflection:
For me, my stroke was the ultimate wake-up call, a stark reminder that ignoring these signs has real, tangible consequences. My body had been trying to communicate with me for years, but I had dismissed its messages as something to "push through." I will never ignore those warning signs again.

Take a moment to write down your own early warning signs. What does exhaustion feel like in your body? What emotional shifts do you notice when you're approaching burnout?

1. What boundaries can I set to protect my energy and well-being?

(Root: Disruption)

Boundaries are not just a luxury, they are a form of protection. Without them, our time, energy, and emotional reserves are at the mercy of external demands. Setting boundaries is a form of disruption, a refusal to perpetuate systems that profit from our overextension.

Consider:
Work boundaries—Can you limit extra responsibilities, set clear working hours, or delegate tasks?
Emotional boundaries—Are there relationships that leave you drained, and how can you minimize exposure or respond differently?
Technology boundaries—Do you need to limit after-hours emails or constant availability to protect your peace?

Personal Reflection:
For years, I struggled to say no, to clients who needed extra time, to colleagues who asked for favors, to institutions that expected my labor without acknowledgment. I feared that setting boundaries would make me seem uncommitted.
But I learned the hard way that overextension is not sustainable. Now, I remind myself that saying no to one thing is saying yes to my well-being.

Identify one boundary you need to set (or reinforce) in your professional or personal life this week. What is one thing you will no longer tolerate?

2. Who or what serves as a source of support and grounding for me?

(Root: Belonging)

Healing does not happen in isolation. Community is one of the most powerful antidotes to burnout and trauma. Belonging is medicine; it regulates the nervous system, reminds us we are not alone, and restores our sense of safety.

Consider:

Personal connections—Who are the people who see you, hold space for you, and remind you of your worth?

Professional networks—Are you connected to other BIPOC clinicians who understand your unique challenges?

Spiritual and ancestral grounding—How do faith, culture, or ancestry serve as a source of strength?

Personal Reflection:

During my most difficult times, I leaned on my people, the ones who reminded me that I did not have to carry it all alone.

My support system includes:

Jevita, who became a sister in healing.

Tee, France, Karen, and my church family at Emmanuel Baptist Church, who lifted me when I felt depleted.

Tommy and my daughters, who reminded me that my worth is not tied to my work, but to my existence.

My sisters, Talanda, Dornesha, and Pashondra, who held me in ways only family can.

Action Step:

Take a moment to write down the names of the people or spaces that make you feel supported. If you struggle to think of any, consider where you can begin cultivating those connections.

CHAPTER 39
ROOT: YIELDING

(Rest, Joy, and the Sacred Pause)

Before we can rest, we must first feel held.

And after community catches us, something quieter rises inside—
a soft invitation from the body that whispers,

"Now that you aren't carrying this alone... you can finally let go."

This is where Yielding begins—

not as collapse,

but as the sacred pause that follows being witnessed. Following the previous chapter on community care and the power of being held, this chapter turns inward, to the sacred act of Yielding.

If Belonging teaches us that we do not heal alone, Yielding teaches us how to soften once we are held.

It is the exhale after the struggle, the pause after the striving, the quiet moment where the body finally believes, *"I am safe enough to rest."*

Yielding is where the nervous system begins to repair.

It is where we remember that rest is not idleness; it is integration.

Joy is a form of resistance.

Rest is a form of reclamation.

Neither should be an afterthought.

Healing cannot be only about survival—it must include pleasure, laughter, and intentional moments of ease.

Consider:

- Daily micro-moments of rest—How can you weave in small, nourishing breaks throughout your day?

- Creative or playful activities—What music, movement, or art brings you joy without obligation?

- Social connection and nature—Who or what makes you feel alive, and how can you make space for that regularly?

Personal Reflection

For too long, I associated joy with guilt, as if resting meant I wasn't *doing enough.*
But my body demanded otherwise.

Now, I sit outside and let the sun warm my skin, grounding myself in the present.
I listen to music that moves me, sometimes dancing, even for a few seconds.
I spend time with my daughters, their laughter reminding me that joy is not frivolous—it is essential. Joy doesn't erase the weight we carry, but it loosens the grip of survival long enough for breath to find us again.
And once joy cracks the door open, even for a moment, we can begin to imagine what daily nourishment might look like.

Action Step

Write down one activity that brings you joy.
How can you integrate it into your day, even for five minutes?

Closing Reflection: Returning to the Roots

Healing is not linear; it spirals.
Each act of care, each boundary, each breath is a return to your roots.

Belonging reminds us that we were never meant to heal alone.
Community, faith, family, and ancestry all hold the medicine of togetherness.

Yielding invites the nervous system to soften, to remember that rest is not weakness but wisdom.

Resilience teaches us that survival is not the same as thriving; it is the quiet strength to rebuild again and again.

Disruption calls us to break the generational pact with exhaustion, to say, *"I will not inherit burnout as my birthright."*

Your self-care, your reflection, your refusal to disappear inside the system, these are not small acts. They are BYRD acts.
Every boundary set, every sigh released, every tear honored, every moment of stillness—each is a note in the liberation song your ancestors began.

So, as you move forward, ask yourself:
Where am I rooted today?
Where am I called to yield?
Where do I need to rise again?
And what must I disrupt to reclaim my peace?

Because your wellness is not an accessory to your work, it is the soil from which your purpose grows.
You are the healer and the healed, the rooted and the rising, the BYRD and the branch.

Resources for Sustaining Wellness

Yielding teaches us how to soften, but sustaining that softness takes intention.

Rest requires structure.

Ease requires tools.

And liberation—real, embodied liberation—requires knowledge.

These resources are not homework.

They are invitations to stay rooted, even when the world pulls at your branches.

The journey to wellness is not a destination; it is a lifelong commitment. As BIPOC clinicians, the need for rest, support, and replenishment is not just personal; it is political.

We are often expected to navigate oppressive systems, provide care to others, and sustain ourselves with little institutional support. Healing, then, becomes an act of defiance, a radical assertion that our well-being is sacred.

At a time when books are being banned, history rewritten, and access to knowledge restricted, we must intentionally seek out the tools that empower us.

Knowledge is not just power; it is liberation. It allows us to name what is happening, reclaim our narratives, and resist the forces that keep us exhausted and uninformed.

1. Readings for Insight and Healing

Books have the power to name what we have experienced, validate our struggles, and illuminate the path toward healing.

Read works that center trauma, rest, resilience, and resistance.

Seek authors who reflect your lived reality and expand your vision for liberation.

Personal Reflection:

There was a time I believed my exhaustion was personal failure rather than systemic consequence. Then I began reading stories that reflected me—Resmaa Menakem, Joy DeGruy, Gabor Maté, Harriet Washington, Deb Dana, Tricia Hersey—and I realized that knowledge could be medicine.

Reading reminded me that rest is not lazy, boundaries are not selfish, and healing is not optional.

Action Step:

Choose one book, article, or documentary this month that speaks to your current struggle or curiosity. Let it teach you something new about how to care for yourself.

2. Professional Networks and Community Support

Healing does not happen in isolation.
As BIPOC clinicians, we thrive when we are seen, heard, and held in community.

Personal Reflection:

For years, I tried to survive in spaces that were never built for me, rooms where my presence was tolerated but not celebrated. I learned that community is not found; it's cultivated. When I connected with networks of other Black and Brown healers, I finally exhaled.

Action Step:

Identify one space—a professional network, peer group, or healing circle—where you feel genuinely seen. If it doesn't exist, consider creating one.

3. Digital Tools for Mindfulness and Regulation

Healing can live in small, digital reminders. Even five minutes of intentional breathwork or guided meditation can interrupt stress patterns.

Look for tools that:

- Center BIPOC voices and culturally rooted healing.
- Offer somatic grounding, breathwork, or gentle guided practices.
- Encourage reflection and consistent nervous system care.

Personal Reflection:
I used to believe that self-care had to be elaborate. Now, I find refuge in simple moments: a five-minute meditation before a session, a mindful breath before logging onto Zoom, or music that softens my chest after a difficult day.

Action Step:
Download one app or digital resource that supports nervous system regulation. Use it consistently, even if only for a few minutes each day.

4. Community-Based Healing Spaces

Healing is collective medicine.
BIPOC professionals often navigate spaces that silence emotion or demand resilience at the expense of humanity.
Community-based healing restores what isolation erodes.

Personal Reflection:
The first time I joined a BIPOC-centered healing circle, I realized I had been carrying my pain in silence. As others spoke their truth, my nervous system finally exhaled. I wept, not from sorrow, but from belonging.

Action Step:
Find or create a healing circle, faith-based group, or ancestral space that allows you to be fully human. Healing shared is healing multiplied.

Closing Reflection: The Right to Know, The Right to Heal

Wellness is not a luxury; it is a birthright.
At a time when truth is under attack, tending to our bodies, minds, and spirits is a revolutionary act.

Ask yourself:
Where do I need more knowledge?
Who must I reach for, and who must I release?
How can I create space for healing today, not tomorrow?

Because Belonging reminds you that you are never alone.
Yielding reminds you that slowing down is sacred.
Resilience reminds you that your survival is a legacy.
Disruption reminds you that liberation begins in your body.

Your rest is resistance.
Your healing is nonnegotiable.
Your wellness is your inheritance.
And every breath you reclaim is a quiet revolution.

Yielding shows us how to rest.
And from that rest, something new begins to rise—
a deeper resilience, a clearer voice, a steadier sense of self.
In the next chapter, we turn toward that rising.
We explore how to build practices that protect our peace, honor our boundaries,
and keep us rooted in liberation even when the world tries to pull us back into survival.

Because Yielding is not the end of the story—
it is the breath that prepares us for what comes next.

INTERLUDE
THE FOUR ROOTS—A RETURN TO OURSELVES

(A Breath Before the Rise)

Healing is not a straight line.
It curves. It circles. It returns us to what we thought we already knew and teaches us to see it again with new eyes.

The BYRD Model carries four roots—not steps, not phases, not skills, but *remembrances*.
They are the places we return to when the world has scattered us into pieces.

These roots showed themselves to me long before I could name them.
They lived in my body, in my breath, in the pauses between collapse and rising.

They live in you, too.

1. Root of Identity—"Who Am I Before the World Told Me Who to Be?"

There is a self beneath the performance.
The self who existed before professionalism, before code-switching, before survival demanded masks.

This root asks:

- Who did you have to become to be allowed in the room?

- Who did you lose along the way?

- Which parts of you have been waiting at the threshold, asking to be let back in?

Identity is not about becoming someone new.
It is the remembering of someone ancient.

2. Root of Story—"What Did I Inherit, and What Am I Done Carrying?"

We are born into chapters already in motion.

Stories of:

- Endurance

- Silence

- being the strong one

- being the one who holds everyone else

Some stories are sacred.
Some were never ours to carry.

This root invites us to:

- release narratives carved from trauma

- reclaim the language of our own lives

To rewrite a story is not to forget.
It is to finally tell the truth in our own voice.

3. Root of Body—"Where Does My Truth Live?"

The body has always known.
Before the words.

Before the insight.
Before the reasoning.

The body keeps score—yes.
But the body also holds the map back home.

This root asks us to listen to:

- the tightening that says no

- the warmth that says stay

- the trembling that says slow down

- the breath that says we survived

Healing does not rush the body.
It waits for the body to soften.

4. Root of System—"What Forces Have Shaped My Pain, and What Must I Refuse?"

We did not create the conditions that harmed us.
We inherited systems built on exhaustion, assimilation, extraction.

This root is not about blame—it is about naming.
Because once something is named, it can no longer pretend to be neutral.

This is the root of:

- Boundaries

- Rest

- Refusal

- reclamation

We stop asking:
"How do I endure this?"

And begin asking:
"What must I lay down to live?"

The Integration

To heal is to let these roots weave back into each other:

- Identity returns us to self.

- Story returns us to meaning.

- Body returns us to presence.

- System returns us to power.

Together, they form the ground beneath the BYRD Model:

Belonging.
Yielding.
Resilience.
Disruption.

Not abstractions.
Not theory.
Not performance.

But lived practice.
Breath by breath.
Moment by moment.
Root by root.

Chapter 40
Being Held: The Medicine of Community

(Root: Belonging)

Community is the drumbeat beneath healing. It says, *You are not alone. You do not have to carry this by yourself.*

For Black and Brown clinicians—who are often holding, guiding, translating, translating again, and making space for others to feel, while rarely being offered space to fall apart—being held is sacred. Necessary. Revolutionary.

This chapter is about the relational soil that allows us to root, soften, replenish, and rise.

I know this in my bones.

My church family at Emmanuel Baptist in San Jose has been a sanctuary. When I had no words, they prayed over me. When I could not hold myself together, they held me. When my faith trembled, they steadied the ground. Their presence did not save me from pain—but it ensured I did not drown in it.

My uncle Alton taught me how to move through rooms with excellence and integrity, not by overperforming, but by remaining myself.

My husband, Tommy, stands beside me with a quiet love that never rushes, never demands, never turns away. Presence as medicine. Soft place to land. Proof that being held is not a luxury; it's life-giving.

And my daughters and grandchildren, who laugh and run and dream so fully, remind me that joy is not something we earn. It is something we inherit, if we make room for it.

Being held is how we survive.
Being held is how we remember ourselves.
Being held is how we come home to our bodies.

When We Learn to Heal Alone

So many of us were raised in homes or systems where being strong was survival.

We learned:

- Don't need too much.

- Don't cry too long.

- Don't break where someone can see it.

- Don't rest unless everything is done, and everything is never done.

Strength became performance.
Care became currency.
Fatigue became identity.

But isolation is erosion.
It eats from the inside out.

My turning point came when my body broke under the weight of being the strong one. After my stroke, I realized I had nothing left to prove, and everything to reclaim.

Healing is not about showing we can endure more.
Healing is about refusing to carry what is killing us.

Reimagining Community: The BYRD Way
Belonging: Who Holds You While You Heal

Belonging is not about matching. It is about being known.

Ask yourself:

- Who sees you without needing you to explain your exhaustion?
- Who listens without rushing to fix?
- Who loves you when you're quiet, tired, undone?

Write their names. Circle them.
These are your people.
Water those relationships.

Yielding: Where Can You Soften?

Yielding is rest as reclamation.
Not collapsing.
Not quitting.

Just lowering the shoulders.
Letting the breath widen.
Trusting you doesn't have to be the scaffolding for everyone else.

Yielding says:
"I deserve to be held, too."

Resilience: Practiced in Community, Not in Isolation

Resilience is not grinding through pain.

Resilience is:

- Asking for help
- Returning to breath
- Allowing joy
- Letting others hold your weight when your knees shake

Resilience grows in relationships that give you back to yourself.

Disruption: Refusing the Lie That Love = Self-Sacrifice

We disrupt harmful patterns when we say:

"No more performing strength.
No more quiet suffering.
No more earning worth."

Disruption is choosing ease where you were taught to choose endurance.

The Grief No One Talks About

When I was healing, some people I believed would show up... did not.

The absence was its own wound.

There is a grief that doesn't involve funerals—
the grief of realizing someone never learned to hold you.

I grieved. I let myself.
And then—I made room for the people who stayed.

Not everyone is meant to walk with us into every season.
Some relationships are complete, even when love remains.

Grief and gratitude can coexist.
Release without bitterness.
Remember without returning.

Building Community With Intention

Ask yourself:

- Where do I feel safe to be my full self?

- Who pours into me without needing to be convinced I'm worth pouring into?

- What relationships feel like exhaling, not bracing?

Choose those.
Let the rest drift like autumn leaves—soft, unforced, returned to
the earth.

Closing Reflection

You were never meant to heal alone.
Your healing does not require shrinking.
Your belonging does not require explanation.

Your softness is not a threat—it is a homecoming.

May you be seen.
May you be held.
May you be rooted in care that does not demand your harm to maintain
connection.

You are the healer and the healed.
You are the soil and the seed.

You are the ancestor in training.
And you are not meant to walk without a hand at your back.

This is where the ancestors lean in,
reminding us that healing begins below the surface.

CHAPTER 41
A VISION FOR THE FUTURE—RECLAIMING SPACE, BODY, AND MIND

Opening Reflection: Healing as Rebellion

Healing is not quiet.
It is not polite.
It does not sit still and wait to be granted permission.

Healing is a declaration.

For Black clinicians and those of the global majority, healing is a direct refusal to be reduced to survival. It is a reclamation of time, breath, softness, joy, rest—all things the world has tried to convince us we have not earned.

Writing this book has taught me that healing is not about returning to who I was before the trauma, before the stroke, before the exhaustion of carrying more than any one body should bear.

It is about becoming the version of myself I never believed I had permission to be.

And that is where this story turns forward.

The Valley: When the World Tries to Define You

As I looked back on my life, I realized healing wasn't asking me to return; it was asking me to re-see the journey that brought me here.

There was a season when I believed healing meant going back, back to the version of me who could push without breaking, who could code-switch with precision, who could carry everyone and still rise early to carry some more.

But going back would mean shrinking again.
Going back would mean silence.
Going back would mean betrayal—of myself.

The world teaches us early:

- Be grateful for what you're given.

- Don't ask for too much.

- You have to be twice as good to be seen as equal.

- You must always endure.

I survived on those lessons—until my body refused to survive like that anymore.

The stroke was not the end.
It was the interruption.
The halting.
The demand.
Sit down. Listen. Live differently.

The Rise: Reclaiming What Was Always Ours

When the old way of surviving collapsed, something new began to take shape, not out of force, but out of necessity.

Healing is not just rest.
Healing is repossession.

Reclaiming Space

We belong in every room our feet touch, and in the rooms we've yet to build.

We are no longer asking for a seat at tables that were never meant
to hold us.
We are crafting new rooms, new tables, new blueprints.

We are building clinics, collectives, community networks where our voices
are not tolerated—they are foundational.

If the institution will not change, we become the institution.

Reclaiming the Body

Our bodies are not machines for labor.
They are living altars.

Liberation looks like:

- Rest without guilt.
- Movement that feels like joy, not discipline.
- Listening to the body when it says "enough."

My Zen room, soft light, grounding textures, the scent of lavender, the
warmth of a weighted blanket, is not luxury.

It is declaration.
I deserve ease.

I deserve softness.
I deserve breath.

Reclaiming the Mind

Oppression does not only harm the body; it colonizes the inner voice.

It teaches us to doubt ourselves, to overwork, to disappear inside our own brilliance.

Therapy gave me language for what I carried.
Affirmations rewrote the script.
Education revealed that my exhaustion had roots outside of me: systemic, historical, inherited.

Liberating the mind is remembering:
I was never the problem.

Collective Healing: Safe Belonging

But healing didn't just happen in solitude or stillness. It deepened in the presence of others, in rooms where my truth was mirrored back to me.

Reflecting on my time with my ATL Somatic Experiencing cohort, I think of how we held one another, without needing to explain, defend, or translate.

The room was filled with BIPOC clinicians carrying their own histories of survival and brilliance.
We understood each other by breath alone.
We honored ancestors with our presence.
We validated one another without hesitation.

That space was a reminder:
Healing is not meant to be done alone.

Returning to the Motherland

And then there were healings that didn't happen in classrooms or circles at all, but on sacred soil my spirit had never forgotten.

Kenya welcomed me like I had been gone a long time but was always expected home.
Egypt spoke through my bones, not in words, but in recognition.
My nervous system exhaled in a way I had never known.

It wasn't learning.
It was remembering.

I realized:

- My story did not begin in trauma.

- My identity is older than violence.

- My body carries memory that predates oppression.

- Belonging is my inheritance.

In Africa, I did not have to earn rest.
Or joy.
Or breath.
I simply was.

The land remembered me, and my body remembered the land.

Section 1:
Empowering Black Clinicians to Liberate the Self

Coming home to myself, through land, lineage, and breath, reshaped how I see the work ahead for all of us.

Liberating the Body

The body is a truth-teller.
When it whispers, we listen.
When it trembles, we stay gentle.
When it asks for rest, we yield.

Movement is no longer something I do to perform strength—
It is something I do to stay alive to myself.

Dancing in the kitchen.
Stretching at sunrise.
Lying still without apology.

Liberating the Mind

Every mirror in my home holds the affirmation:
I am enough.

Not because I earned it.
Not because I proved it.
But because I am.

Therapy became ritual.
Learning became armor.
Self-trust became return.

Liberating Space

My spaces reflect my soul now:

- Elephant figurines for wisdom and memory.
- Butterflies for emergence and new wings.
- Candles for breath.
- Green plants for life still growing.

My Zen room is not décor.
It is reclamation.

Envisioning a Future of Collective Liberation

And once we reclaim our inner landscape, the vision of what we can build together becomes undeniable.

I imagine:
A mental health field shaped by those who have been harmed by it, and therefore will heal it differently.

I imagine:
Training programs led by Black women, queer therapists, immigrant healers, Indigenous knowledge holders.

I imagine:
Rooms where our voices are not the exception, they are the standard.

This is not fantasy.
It is blueprint.
And we are already building it.

Closing Reflection: The Elephant and the Butterfly

All of this—the remembering, the returning, the rising—leads me here, to the truth held in two sacred symbols...

The elephant is memory, lineage, rootedness.
The butterfly is transformation, emergence, ascension.

I am both now.
So are you.

We carry what we have survived, and we rise beyond it.
We remember where we come from, and we claim where we are going.

Healing is not about returning to what was.
It is about becoming who we were always meant to be.

So as you step forward, ask yourself:
What am I reclaiming?
What am I releasing?
Who am I becoming?

Because your healing is not small.
It is not private.
It is not quiet.

Your healing is a revolution.
And you are ready.

We rise, elephants steady, butterflies soaring.
Our trauma becomes our gift.
Our healing becomes our legacy.
Our future becomes our freedom.

References

Alexander, M. (2012). *The new Jim Crow: Mass incarceration in the age of colorblindness.* The New Press.

Dana, D. (2018). *Polyvagal exercises for safety and connection: 50 client-centered practices.* W. W. Norton.

DeGruy, J. (2017). *Post traumatic slave syndrome: America's legacy of enduring injury and healing.* Joy DeGruy Publications.

Haines, S. K. (2019). *The politics of trauma: Somatics, healing, and social justice.* North Atlantic Books.

Hannah-Jones, N. (2021). *The 1619 Project: A new origin story.* One World.

Hersey, T. (2022). *Rest is resistance: A manifesto.* Little, Brown Spark.

Kain, K. L., & Terrell, S. (2018). *Nurturing resilience: Helping clients move from stuckness to thriving.* W. W. Norton.

Levine, P. A. (1997). *Waking the tiger: Healing trauma.* North Atlantic Books.

Maté, G. (2003). *When the body says no: Exploring the stress-disease connection.* Vintage Canada.

Maté, G. (2022). *The myth of normal: Trauma, illness, and healing in a toxic culture.* Avery.

McDaniel, K. (2021). *Mother hunger: How adult daughters can understand and heal from lost nurturance, protection, and guidance.* Hay House.

Menakem, R. (2017). *My grandmother's hands: Racialized trauma and the pathway to mending our hearts and bodies.* Central Recovery Press.

Menakem, R. (2022). *The quaking of America: An embodied guide to navigating our nation's upheaval and reshaping our collective future.* Central Recovery Press.

Pittman, C. M., & Karle, E. M. (2015). *Rewire your anxious brain: How to use the neuroscience of fear to end anxiety, panic, and worry.* New Harbinger.

Porges, S. W. (2011). *The polyvagal theory: Neurophysiological foundations of emotions, attachment, communication, and self-regulation.* W. W. Norton.

Roisin, F. (2022). *Who is wellness for? An examination of wellness culture and who it leaves behind.* Harper Wave.

Shim, R. S., & Vinson, S. Y. (2023). *Social (in)justice and mental health.* American Psychiatric Association Publishing.

Tisby, J. (2019). *The color of compromise: The truth about the American church's complicity in racism.* Zondervan.

Washington, H. A. (2006). *Medical apartheid: The dark history of medical experimentation on Black Americans from colonial times to the present.* Doubleday.

Williams, T. M. (2008). *Black pain: It just looks like we're not hurting.* Scribner.

About the Author

Sharlisa Byrd, LMFT, SEP, TITC-CT, CCHt is a Licensed Marriage and Family Therapist, Certified Clinical Traumatologist, Somatic Experiencing Practitioner, Certified Clinical Hypnotherapist, and Adjunct Professor at the University of San Francisco. She is known for her ability to hold complexity with compassion, weaving together trauma science, somatic healing, ancestral wisdom, and cultural liberation in ways that are accessible, embodied, and transformative.

Born in New Orleans, Louisiana, and raised on the vibrant, complicated streets of San Francisco, Sharlisa carries the resilience, brilliance, and spiritual grounding of Black Southern roots blended with the grit and innovation of the Bay Area. Her work sits at the intersection of racialized trauma, nervous system regulation, and somatic liberation for Black and Brown clinicians who are called to heal in systems that were never built for them.

Her professional journey has been shaped by her years as a trauma specialist, her own lived experiences navigating systemic injustice, and her personal healing following a stroke caused by chronic workplace stress. This rupture became a turning point, one that called her back to her body, her lineage, and the sacred work of reclaiming rest, belonging, and liberation as acts of rebellion.

Sharlisa teaches graduate-level counseling courses across multiple campuses of the University of San Francisco, where she is known for her warmth, humor, poetic teaching style, and ability to hold a room with both tenderness and truth. She specializes in Somatic Experiencing, EMDR, trauma-informed care, anti-oppressive practice, and somatic abolitionism.

She is the founder of Byrd's Eye View Professional Counseling Solutions, a healing-centered practice dedicated to helping individuals and clinicians reconnect with their bodies, reclaim their stories, and cultivate resilience grounded in culture and nervous system wisdom.

Outside the therapy room, Sharlisa is a mother of six daughters and grandmother to three beautiful granddaughters, her "butterflies," and a wife to her beloved husband, Tommy, whose quiet strength and unwavering presence helped guide her back to herself. Her family is her grounding force, her joy, and the living proof of the transformation she teaches.

Healing the Healers is her first book—a love letter, a blueprint, and a liberation map for every Black and Brown clinician who has ever held the world together while their own body trembled beneath the weight.

Afterward

The wear and tear of racist enactments in the "mental health" field is an abomination. Sharlisa Byrd has found her way to reclaim her wellness by following anti-racist somatic leaders and synthesizing their teachings into her own approach. She offers herself and her wisdom rooted in Love for your well-being and your compassion satisfaction. May you receive her Love and let it support your integration of all that this world has asked you to carry, and may it help you lay your burden down. May her encouragement help you find safe places, people, and practices to help you digest and rest.

Karen Roller

Appendix A— Resources for Healing, Liberation, and Embodied Care

A Closing Companion for Clinicians of the Global Majority

Healing is not a task—it is a lifelong return.

A return to the body, to lineage, to breath, to truth.

These resources exist as guides, mirrors, and companions for the journey.

May they nourish you the way breath nourishes a tired chest, the way community steadies trembling hands, the way ancestral memory softens the ground beneath your feet.

Recommended Reading for Clinicians

Texts that illuminate trauma, resilience, rest, and liberation

Somatic & Body-Based Healing

Dana, Deb — *Polyvagal Exercises for Safety and Connection*

Kain, K. L., & Terrell, S. — *Nurturing Resilience*

Levine, P. — *Waking the Tiger*

Porges, S. — *The Polyvagal Theory*

Pittman, C. M., & Karle, E. — *Rewire Your Anxious Brain*

Racial Trauma, Oppression & Collective Healing

Menakem, R. — *My Grandmother's Hands*

Menakem, R. — *The Quaking of America*

DeGruy, J. — *Post Traumatic Slave Syndrome*

Haines, S. — *The Politics of Trauma*

Washington, H. — *Medical Apartheid*

Rest, Identity & Self-Reclamation

Hersey, T. — *Rest Is Resistance*

McDaniel, K. — *Mother Hunger*

Maté, G. — *The Myth of Normal*

Maté, G. — *When the Body Says No*

Williams, T. M. — *Black Pain*

Systems, Justice & Cultural Context

Alexander, M. — *The New Jim Crow*

Hannah-Jones, N. — *The 1619 Project*

Shim, R. S., & Vinson, S. Y. — *Social (In)Justice and Mental Health*

Tisby, J. — *The Color of Compromise*

Roisin, F. — *Who Is Wellness For?*

Somatic Modalities for Continued Healing

Practices that connect the nervous system to resilience and repair

Somatic Experiencing (SE)

Supports renegotiation of trauma by working gently with the body's natural rhythms.

Polyvagal-Informed Approaches

Cultivates ventral vagal safety, relational trust, and nervous system stability.

Somatic Abolitionism

Embodied healing of racialized trauma through ancestral presence, community repair, and grounded refusal.

Trauma-Sensitive Mindfulness

Nonforceful attention that protects against overwhelm and honors pacing.

Breath-Based Practices

Exhale-focused, noncounted breathing, humming, and grounding breaths that regulate without pressure.

Movement & Embodied Expression

Shaking, stretching, dancing, swaying—restoring flow where trauma created freeze.

Cultural & Ancestral Somatics

Practices rooted in lineage, ritual, and ancestral memory that honor identity and belonging.

Liberation & Ancestral Healing: A Starter Library

Books that restore context, culture, and collective truth

The 1619 Project — reframing history with honesty and depth.
Post Traumatic Slave Syndrome — situating modern trauma in historical context.
My Grandmother's Hands — a somatic lens on racialized trauma.
The Quaking of America — navigating cultural crisis with embodied grounding.
The Politics of Trauma — reclaiming trauma work from individualism.
Rest Is Resistance — remembering that rest is a birthright.
The Color of Compromise — exposing historical structures of harm.
Medical Apartheid — documenting medical exploitation across

generations.

Black Pain — naming the emotional truths of Black experience.

Closing Blessing for the Healer

May these teachings become:

- the breath you return to,

- the ground beneath your feet,

- the whisper reminding you that you belong to yourself,

- and the map back home when the world feels too heavy.

Your healing is not a luxury
it is lineage work,
liberation work,
and love in motion.

Appendix B—Somatic Exercises for Black & Brown Clinicians

Tools to unwind, return, and restore

These practices honor the body as a living archive—one that holds both generational pain *and* ancestral wisdom. Each exercise is gentle, culturally attuned, and designed for clinicians navigating the layered stress of oppression, emotional labor, and holding space for others.

1. The Grounded Throne (Belonging)

A reminder that your body has a home.

How to practice:

1. Sit back in your chair, allowing your spine to soften.
2. Place both feet on the floor—let them feel claimed by the earth.
3. Press your thighs gently into the seat; let the chair hold you.
4. Inhale and feel your ribs widen; exhale and let your shoulders drop.
5. Whisper: *I belong in this body. I belong in this moment.*

Why It Works:
Grounding the pelvis and back signals safety to the nervous system, counteracting vigilance rooted in racism and chronic survival mode.

2. Rocking as Rhythm (Yielding)

A return to the ancient movements that soothed generations.

How to practice:

1. Sit or stand comfortably.

2. Begin slow, rhythmic side-to-side rocking.

3. Let breath follow naturally—no counting, no force.

4. Add a soft hum if it feels good.

Why It Works:
Rocking is one of the earliest co-regulation patterns we experience—it invites the body out of threat and into rest.

3. The Tremor Release (Resilience)

Shaking to complete what the body could not finish.

How to practice:

1. Stand with knees soft and feet hip-distance apart.

2. Begin shaking your hands.

3. Let the movement build—arms, shoulders, hips, legs.

4. Allow yawns, sighs, tears, or laughter.

5. End by placing a hand over your heart.

Why It Works:
Shaking discharges survival energy and resets the autonomic nervous system.

4. The Boundary Breath (Disruption)

Breathing that honors your limits, not your labor.

How to practice:

1. Inhale through the nose.

2. Exhale with a soft "hmmm" sound.

3. Feel the vibration in your throat and chest.

4. Say quietly: *"No more shrinking."*

Why It Works:
The hum stimulates the vagus nerve and reinforces self-protection.

5. Ancestral Spine Alignment (Lineage Connection)

For clinicians carrying generational weight.

How to practice:

1. Sit tall and imagine a long line extending down your spine.

2. Visualize ancestors placing a gentle hand at your back.

3. Breathe into the vertical length of your body.

4. Whisper: *I come from survivors.*

Why It Works:
Imagery + somatic alignment strengthens internal stability and embodied identity.

Appendix C—BYRD Model Worksheets

Reflection tools for restoring power,
softening survival, and rebuilding self-trust.

Worksheet 1—Belonging Inventory

Where do I feel most held?

Prompts:

- Three people who see me without performance:
- Spaces where my breath naturally slows:
- What belonging feels like in my body:
- Where belonging is missing—and why:

Worksheet 2—Yielding Scan

Where can I soften?

Questions:

- What signs tell me I need to slow down?
- How does my body show fatigue?
- What rest practices feel truly nourishing?
- One thing I can release this week:

Worksheet 3—Resilience Reality Check

What supports my rise?

Prompts:

- Practices that return me to myself:
- My early warning signs of burnout:
- Who I can reach out to when I'm overwhelmed:
- A resilience practice I want to deepen:

Worksheet 4—Disruption Map

What must change for me to heal?

Prompts:

- Boundaries I've been afraid to set:
- Places I'm shrinking to make others comfortable:
- Systems or relationships draining my energy:
- A disruption I commit to this month:

Worksheet 5—Four Roots Reflection

Identity—Who was I before survival shaped me?
Story—What am I done carrying?
Body—What truth is my body speaking right now?
System—What must I refuse to absorb?

Appendix D—Pelvic Floor Exercises for Trauma Recovery

Gentle, culturally informed practices for clinicians whose bodies carry lived trauma.

Your pelvic floor is not just muscle—it is memory.
It holds fear, bracing, shame, and survival... but also pleasure, power, grounding, and ancestral wisdom.

These practices are noninvasive, nontriggering, and Somatic Experiencing-aligned.

1. The Soft Belly Drop

For releasing bracing and hypervigilance.

How to practice:

1. Place one hand on your lower belly.
2. Take a soft inhale.
3. On the exhale, imagine the belly dropping like warm sand.
4. Let the pelvic floor melt downward.

2. The Supported Hip Opener

To release long-held tension.

How to practice:

1. Sit cross-legged or with feet together.

2. Place pillows under knees for support.

3. Inhale length; exhale soften.

4. Notice any trembling—allow it.

3. Micro-Release Pulses

To reconnect to safety without forcing sensation.

How to practice:

1. Imagine the pelvic floor lifting 10 percent.

2. Release it gently.

3. Repeat 5–10 times.

4. Stop immediately if any discomfort arises.

4. The Pelvic Bowl Visualization

For reclaiming agency over the pelvic space.

How to practice:

1. Visualize a glowing bowl in your pelvis.

2. Fill it with warmth, ancestry, light.

3. Let it overflow down your legs and up your spine.

5. Supported Child's Pose Variation

For grounding the lower body.

How to practice:

1. Kneel and fold forward onto stacked pillows.

2. Let knees widen—but only within comfort.

3. Allow breath to widen the back and hips.

Appendix E—Daily Nervous System Regulation Journal

Use this as a living document—a daily conversation between you and your body.

Morning Check-In

- Today my body feels:
- My emotional weather:
- What I need more of:
- What I need less of:

Midday Pause

- What shifted in my body today?
- One thing that felt nourishing:
- One thing that felt draining:
- A boundary I honored (or wish I had):

Evening Release

- What tension am I holding?
- What helped me regulate today?
- What gratitude does my body want to express?
- A moment of joy, even a small one:

Weekly Reflection

- One thing I'm proud of this week:
- One pattern I noticed:
- One thing I'm ready to let go of:
- One place I want to disrupt exhaustion: